SAINTS
FOR
CONFUSED
TIMES

SAINTS
FOR
CONFUSED
TIMES

by
John Garvey

THE THOMAS MORE PRESS
Chicago, Illinois

ISBN 0-88347-066-7

CONTENTS

For My Grandparents

PREFACE

This is not a book of biographies. For lives of the saints you would do well to see Butler's *Lives*, or the dictionaries of saints edited by Donald Attwater and John Coulson. What I offer here are meditations which grew from reflection on the lives of some saints, and they are offered in the conviction that what saints in every age have lived through (and what they lived for) speaks as much to our age as any. Two ideas are dominant here. One is something which the Fathers of the Church called "deification," the process by which we are transformed into what Christ is. The other is whole-heartedness. The saints, finally, were undivided; they were whole. Kierkegaard's belief that "purity of heart is to think one thing" applies to them.

A priest once wrote a book about humility and then urged it on everyone he knew as the best work ever written on the subject. Remembering this I have to confess an embarrassment at writing a book about saints, a project which is certainly amusing to my wife, friends, and other people who know me. I can only steal a line from John of the ladder, a seventh century hermit, quoted by Henri Nouwen in *Reaching Out:* "If some are still dominated by their former bad habits, and yet can teach by mere words, let them teach. . . . For perhaps, being put to shame by their own words, they will eventually begin to practice what they teach."

—John Garvey

INTRODUCTION

Two quotes, first. Athanasius wrote, "The Word became man so that men might become gods." And Irenaeus wrote, "The glory of God is man, fully realized."

These two quotes point to one truth: Man fully realized is more than man, is in some way divine. What we are given in God's generosity is not merely redemption from sin and illusion, but a share in the life of God. In the West, Christians have paid more attention to the idea that God is the one who judges and rewards or punishes our actions, than to the God who invites us to share divine life. Consequently, our idea of a good life is one which involves behavior more than the heart, and so we see the saints as people whose standards of behavior were much better than our own, whose actions reflected their dedication perfectly; where our own actions at best give weak waves in the direction of what we claim to believe, or acknowledge it by not contradicting it *too* blatantly.

It is not that we never think of sanctity as a heartfelt thing, but more frequently it is regarded as something ethical—an absolute ethical goodness, compared to our qualified, relative goodness. This leads us into illusions about ourselves as well as the saints, and it lets us miss something which eventually came to be at the center of every saint's life.

That is, the belief—the knowledge—that God is real.

It is shocking to consider the possibility that I really do not believe in God's reality. But it has to be faced. Some people who face it conclude that they do not believe, and that's the end of it. There is probably more courage and honesty in that conclusion than in the sort of belief which is little more than limp acquiescence to tradition. Most of us are Christians because our parents raised us that way. Even for Christians who think a lot about being Christian, religion becomes an ethical system founded on the idea of God's existence, and by talking rather easily of the replacement of the old law by the new law we imply that Christianity meant the replacement of one code of ethics with another (an idea which is unfair to both Christianity and Judaism).

What has happened here is that our culture has told us something about a being called God, and we respond by saying that we believe in the stories we have heard, or that we do not. Either way, we try to offer ourselves more or less decent reasons for our belief or the lack of it. If we are believers, we go through the rituals and obey the ethical codes (or try to) which have been handed on as appropriate for believers.

The problem with this is that while it can be the beginning of a relationship with God, it can also serve as a barrier to such a relationship. In her fine novel *The Man on a Donkey* (Macmillan, 1952) H.F.M. Prescott describes a crucifix on the wall of a reformation-era room as the image of a tormented man nailed to a tree, and she says that the

people in the room live comfortably with it because "they knew it too well to see it for what it
was." This is the barrier which organized religion
presents to the gospel—the very thing it is called
upon to preach becomes a convention; it is brought
down to the level it was meant to raise us from, so
that we can live comfortably with it, which is
precisely what we are *not* meant to do.

But there are times in the lives of most believers
when suddenly the words of the gospel, words
they have heard all their lives, take on a strange
sound. Familiar words are disturbing: "Leave all
you have and follow me." "He who seeks his life
will lose it, and he who loses his life will find it."
What you do to the least of these, my brothers, you
do to me." "Love one another, as I have loved
you." Then we ask ourselves: How would I live if
those words were real for me? The abstraction
into which we usually force God vanishes for a
moment, and the reality of God, or the possibility
of God's reality, touches us, raising disturbing
questions. Does my life remotely answer the challenge these words suggest? God's reality can begin
to touch us when we realize our cold-heartedness
in the face of the fact that there is "nothing in all
creation that can separate us from the love of God
in Jesus Christ our Lord."

It is not enough to let the questions bother us, or
to consider them as interesting (Sometimes theology seems to proclaim: "The Word became
interesting, and dwelt among us.") Anthony
Bloom writes: "The realm of God is dangerous.

You must enter into it and not just seek information about it" (*Beginning to Pray,* Paulist, 1970).
The more whole-hearted our belief in God's reality,
the more whole-hearted will we be about responding to it. Not to respond at all means a refusal to
admit that God's desire for us is real—which
means a denial that God is real. To the degree that
we do not respond we do not really believe that
God is Lord of all.

Saints are people who have seen through the
idol we usually make of God to the knowledge that
God is real. That transformation always involves
ethical behavior and moral action to some extent,
but it involves much more than that—it involves a
wholeheartedness which is central to being Christian, not just to being a saint. Saints are people
whose ambition is to be saints, or to fit into any
other human definition. They simply want to be
what God wants them to be.

To find out what this means for our time, we
have to see what it has meant in the past, in the
lives of men and women recognized as saints.
Some of them look larger than life, and show a
surprising depth of humanity. It is surprising
partly because we are not accustomed to thinking
of saints as people of deep and abiding passion,
but it is surprising also because we are not accustomed to seeing that depth in anyone. It is at
once attractive and repellent. "Nude bodies no
longer shock us," Shaw wrote in a completely different context, "but the disgust aroused by a
naked soul is intolerable." There is something

naked about the saints: They were willing to be
seen and judged by others without the fear most of
us have revealing those things which matter very
much to us. They were willing to be vulnerable in
this way because they had accepted their reality
from God, and they were not worried about the
world's definition of what matters and what does
not.

This brings us back to the quotes at the beginning: Divinity was beginning to show itself in them.
Peter tells us that we are to become "partakers of
the divine nature," and Paul speaks of Jesus as
"the firstborn of the new men". Human nature, as
God wills it to be, is what Jesus' nature is. Baptism
is the sign that we have been called to die and rise
with Christ, and this activity is the real life of
Christians. This dying and rising is given: It is not
something we can accomplish by any effort, but
we have to attend to it, watch for it, be faithful to
it.

The saints are examples of what it means to pay
that attention. They are not always sympathetic or
comfortable, but their involvement is always total.
Their example should not make us want to be "like
them" in the imitative sense. It should lead us to
examine ourselves. When Paul says, "each man
should examine his own conduct for himself; then
he can measure his achievement by comparing
himself with himself, and not anyone else," this
applies to the comparisons we might be tempted to
make between the quality of our own lives and the
lives of the saints. We should examine ourselves in

the light of their commitment not by comparing
lives—it is God and not the saints we are called to
follow. But the God we confess belief in is usually
rather abstract, or else he is an image made in our
likeness. God says of David that David is a man
after God's own heart, and this is what everyone
is called to be. The saints (like David) were friends
of God. They responded personally, in love, completely, as a friend responds to a friend or lover to
lover. This response can overcome the narrow-
ness of our imagination. Once we accept the idea
that God is more real than we are, "nearer to us
than we are to ourselves," as Augustine said, then
we can begin to learn from those who lived the
consequences of that knowledge.

While it is true that there is a danger in
stressing experience in the religious life—the experience, for example, of feeling sure that God
loves you or has forgiven you, or the experience of
certainty beyond any doubt that God exists—in the
long run we are asked to know God in a way that
will include experience. This might include the experience of darkness, of feeling completely abandoned by God, or feeling empty of every emotion,
every desire to love God or man. But it also includes
the realization, which is more than an idea, that
even these are given things, not merely moods. It
is not enough to accept the idea that God exists, or
to live ethically with that idea in mind. I realize
that this is contrary to much that Christians have
come to believe of religion, but looking at the lives
of men and women who have acknowledged as

having lived the Christian life well, we see that the experience of God was frequently a vital thing in their growth toward God. I am not speaking now of the mystical experience of union with God, but rather of the fact that they felt constantly in dialogue with him. The religious life for the saint was not just a matter of obeying the rules, or doing good things.

Karl Rahner said in an interview that as helpful as enthusiastic forms of Christianity can be (he was speaking of the charismatic movement), many people by virtue of their temperaments must be content with what he called a "more wintery" form of spirituality. The phrase is a good one and the idea is correct, as anyone who has ever been annoyed by "born again" Christians will attest, when they push for a lightning flash form of belief which most of us are incapable of, for good skeptical reasons. But even if we acknowledge that our faith should not be *based* upon experience, there is an element of experience which is important to faith. It is a kind of attention which waits, and which finally leads us to see things in a new light, an attention to those occasions of dying and rising which happen in our lives, an attention which over the years leads us to understand that we are led, despite our thickheadedness, toward the life which God intends for us. This is not always blindingly apparent, and if a person refuses to do the waiting and watching it will not be apparent at all. And it is true that some people, waiting and watching, might feel that they are spending their whole lives

in a darkness with no light in sight. Still, the
willingness to wait, the desire to know God, to be
made into the sort of person who can look upon
God's face and live, is the point. It must become a
search for us, and not just a code of ethics. If it is
not a search for God it is not really God we believe
in, but the idea of God. The God which Jewish and
Christian tradition presents is a mystery present
in every moment. Not to look for God is to deny
God. We are advised to seek the kingdom of God,
and this cannot be a matter of mere intellectual
assent.

The Hasidic master Barukh of Medzebozh put it
this way: "Imagine two children playing hide-and-
seek; one hides but the other does not look for him.
God is hiding and man is not seeking. Imagine His
distress" (Elie Wiesel, *Souls on Fire*, Random
House, 1972). That *looking for* God is the experience the saints opened themselves to, wholeheartedly. We are on the other side of that opening.
Watching them we may come to understand what
it would mean to undertake the life God offers.

*   *   *

The word "saint" has gone through a number of
changes in Christian history. In the beginning,
saints were those whose radical decision to be
Christian separated them from the world; they
were being made over again, they participated
in the new creation which Christ's resurrection
and ascension and the presence of the Holy Spirit
heralded. Later the saints were the martyrs of the

early churches, revered first by the local Christian community, and then by other churches. Ascetics were included later, following the persecutions. They were included because their abandonment of the things the world offered was understood as an important part of the dying to self which Jesus asked of his followers. Finally the definition of sanctity grew broad enough to include Christians whose lives showed that they had taken the words of the gospel to heart so completely that those words became flesh in them.

Different criteria have been used at different times to determine who the saints were. At first a locally celebrated saint was simply accepted as a saint by the church—the process was one of acclamation. Later the process of canonization became a very formal thing, and the Roman Catholic and Eastern Orthodox churches still have formal approaches to the acknowledgement of sainthood.

It isn't the purpose of this book to deal with the formal apparatus surrounding sainthood. What I would like to point out here is that throughout the history of Christianity the acknowledgement of saints and of the idea of sanctity has been a central part of the Christian life. The Protestant reformation, reacting against the many abuses which had crept into the church's approach to saints and their veneration, rejected the idea of saints as idolatrous. The idea had to be jettisoned if the church were ever to return to the purity of the gospels. In recent years, the idea has also lost some of its former place in Catholicism. But if the saints were what Christians for most of Christian history said they were—that is, the Christians who took the gospel to heart and revealed to us what it means to live Christ's life—then the concept has to be restored.

Saints should unsettle us, as prophets do. Despite the differences between the ages in which they lived and our own age, they should become contemporary enough to force us to examine the way in which we regard Christianity. That is the purpose of this book: The decisions, the deeds, and the understandings which went to make up the lives of the saints illuminate something of the mystery of Christ—the Christ who is a God of the living. And perhaps this concept, that God is a God of the living, can shed some light on the phrase repeated every Sunday in the creed: The proclamation of our belief in the communion of saints.

Without this belief we can easily become idolatrous. We can idolize an age (the age of the apostles) or a way of life (the life of the respectable citizen, the churchgoer). The tendency towards idolizing particular eras in church history is common, and it must be admitted that the presence of saints in every era did not prevent counter-reformation Catholicism from idolizing the 13th century. The current tendency seems to be the idolization of the pre-Constantinian age, especially the church we see in the Acts of the Apostles. A look at saints throughout the history of the church can show the range of Christian possibilities. There were establishment saints like Thomas More and anti-establishment saints like Francis of Assisi. There have been soldier saints and pacifist saints, saints who all their lives were pious and saints who began as whores and gamblers. Some saints were deeply contemplative. Others, though prayerful, were concerned primarily with service to the poor. Looking at the range of lives which they lived we can arrive at an openness to the changes which have occurred throughout Christian history; and this in turn could bring us to an openness to change which we, maybe more than any other generation of Christians, will be called upon to understand. It will keep our understanding of change from being so open-ended that no "discernment of spirits" is possible, and it will also keep us from being unreceptive to the possible manifestations of the Spirit in our time. Without an attempt at understanding the saints a knowledge of Christian history can make us open but academic, and distant—again the danger is that of seeking information about the kingdom of God, without knowing what it means to enter it.

It is important *not* to see in the saint the equivalent of the class called by some gnostic sects "perfectly," the perfect ones. Those sects divided their religion into two main groups: The "Perfect", who had accepted the message fully and were different in kind from the other group, the "Believers," who believed but were not yet willing to take on the burdens of belief. Christianity may look like this sometimes—certainly those who have not given away all they have, who have not died to self, should be hesitant in calling themselves Christian; but the irony involved in Christianity is that no one, finally, is able to say those things of himself. Where the saints differ from "ordinary believers" is something visible to everyone but the saints themselves, who usually thought of themselves as profoundly unworthy. The "Perfect" know that they were perfect, but the saint does not feel that way. The saints did not aim at "being saints" but at following Christ, at being daughters and sons of the God they met in Jesus. They took the gospel to heart; they did not do anything more than they knew to be necessary. They simply tried to live the beatitudes.

When we hear the words, "God is a God of the living," we can interpret them in a very traditional way: Those who love God live on in God even through death; everyone who believes in God will be saved. This is certainly an essential part of Christian belief, but there is another way to regard those words which may be more directly challenging. They can remind us forcefully that the time we have been given is *this moment*, and there is never any other. We are the living Jesus talks about when he speaks of the "God of the living," and so are the saints. This should lead to a consideration of the degree to which we respond (or fail to respond) to the life which God offers us, new, every moment. Looking at the lives of the saints can tell us about the God they served, the

God we are called to serve, the God who lives, not at all in our ideas of him, but in the moments we live through. We might begin to understand that God is real, which could lead to other beginnings.

Chapter One

Francis of Assisi

There is probably no saint as appealing to so many people as Francis of Assisi. He has been called the saint who is most like Christ. Even in the wild company of the saints his literal acceptance of the gospel stands out. But much of the appreciation of Francis has been sentimental, and it ignores aspects of his life which are difficult to understand and not very sympathetic. The popular picture of Francis is one of unrelieved pleasantness: He was an advocate of simple living who gathered like-minded Christians around him; he was good to animals, could talk to them and tame them; everyone liked him.

It is true that early accounts of Francis' life stress his attractiveness to many people, people who might have found another person insane, if he were to act the way Francis did. And the taming of the wolf of Gubbio and Francis' sermon to the birds are stories which circulated within a couple of generations of the first Franciscans. There must be some truth to the pleasant picture of Francis which has come down to us.

Here, however, we are confronted with the same problem Jesus poses. Our tendency is to look only at the Jesus who was kind to children and sinners, and not the severe Jesus, the one who was quick to expose hypocrisy, drive money-lenders from the temple, whose behavior to his mother and his followers seems at times abrupt, if not rude. However likeable Francis was, however tender, there is another and more paradoxical facet of his life which may be more important to an understanding of Francis. It may be more important because if it is true that Francis was like Christ, the vital point is not to emphasize those virtues which everyone understands, but those strange things which almost nobody understands, and hardly anyone likes. We love the Francis who was kind, and the Francis who composed hymns to the sun is marvelous; but it is hard to feel near to the Francis who stripped himself naked to show his independence from his family, or who threw himself into thorn bushes. Francis was, in worldly terms, uncompromising and unrealistic. When his followers asked for some of the security every other religious order knew, he was furious. Although by the time he died he was loved by thousands, during the time immediately following his conversion he was considered mad and was beaten by people who were offended by his rags and his eccentric behavior.

It is this Francis we must try to understand—the fool for Christ, who said that the passion and humiliation of Jesus were all the instruction he needed.

The notion of becoming a fool for Christ's sake goes back to the passage in the gospel where Jesus rejoiced that God had revealed his truth to the simple and had hidden it from those the world calls wise; and the theme is taken up by Paul, who calls the cross a scandal because it contradicts the wisdom of the world . . . it is folly. John Saward writes (in *The Fool for Christ's Sake in Monasticism*, John Saward, an essay in *Theology and Prayer*, The Fellowship of St. Alban and St. Sergius, 1975), "The most important characteristic of the fools, the basis and inspiration of all that they do and are, is identity with Christ crucified, their participation in the poverty, nakedness, humiliation, and abandonment of the Lord, and here the spirit of folly for Christ's sake comes close to the spirit of martyrdom." Saward quotes Kologrivov, who writes that the basis of the fool's vocation "is the awareness of the soul's terrible responsibility towards God," a responsibility which consists of "taking voluntarily on oneself humiliations and insults, in order to increase humility, meekness, and kindness of heart, and so to develop love, even for one's enemies and persecutors."

The fool for Christ's sake has appeared again and again in Christian history. In Russia it became a kind of charismatic institution. Saward mentions the fact that Russian fools for Christ usually appeared as pilgrims, who frequently offended the pious. St. Basil the Blessed stole the merchandise of dishonest tradesmen, stoned the houses of the respectable, wept with sinners, and denounced the injustice of the czar. He once offered Ivan the Terrible a piece of raw meat; Ivan refused, and Basil then showed him in the sky the souls of innocent people Ivan had murdered. In the West the same phenomen occurred. St. Philip Neri shaved

half of his beard off, wore his coat inside out,
walked past the Tabernacle without genuflecting;
and like Basil he combined this with a sense of
social justice, working to prevent gypsies from
being used as galley slaves by the papal fleet.
Following his conversion, St. John of God was considered a lunatic, and there are numerous other
examples of this strange way of responding to the
gospel.

Of course we have to consider the possibility
that such people really were mad. But as easy as
this judgment might be in the case of some saints
whose behavior strikes us as outrageous (Chris-
tina the Astonishing, for example, whose weird
behavior is frankly described as schizophrenic by
her most recent Catholic biographers), it doesn't
hold up for others. St. Basil's mad behavior before
the Czar told a truth which the more restrained
sanity of the "respectable" did not dare to tell.
The gospel reveals things hidden from the beginning of time, and the uncovering of those things
can lead to strange behavior—Bartimaeus calls
out to Jesus for mercy, while his embarrassed
companions try to silence him; Zaccheus climbs a
tree to get a glimpse of Jesus, leaving respectability behind. What the world considers crazy
makes sense in this context.

It is not possible to retain both our sense of
having an easy place in this world and the notion
that we are following Christ. Kierkegaard calls the
desire to maintain respectability and worldly
honor while calling oneself a Christian "wanting

to have a mouthful of flour, and to blow." Jesus said that his followers were to leave all they had behind, not looking back; he said that following him meant taking up the cross daily, and dying to self. What this means will vary, life to life. But what it does *not* mean is peace, as the world gives it. It does not mean an easy life, or a life which is at home in any society. To the extent that we are willing to serve both God and Mammon we are not followers of Christ; and we are not, in fact, following God at all. Jesus did not say that it is undesirable to follow God and Mammon. He said you *cannot* do it. What you serve is not God, but an idol of the same name, as long as your allegiance is half-hearted.

In writing this way I have to be careful; I can't claim to have made the move Jesus asks of us. I may have met one or two people who have. At best I'm a fellow-traveler, sympathetic, not yet completely committed. Perhaps this is why we are more comfortable calling ourselves "Catholic," "Anglican," "Protestant" than we are calling ourselves "Christian." And this may be why we are uncomfortable around those who "get saved," who are easy about calling themselves Christians, or who claim that their commitment is total. Our embarrassment is not, as the saved sometime seem to think, that we have not made their noble decision. It is rather a feeling of embarrassment for them, because what they say is obviously not the truth.

Faced with this common discomfort—a discomfort around those who say that they are saved, and a discomfort at our own lives, since we do not live what we profess to believe—we can respond in a number of ways. It seems to me that the least healthy is to seek a means of making ourselves feel committed without having to change our lives in any but an emotional way, through involvement with enthusiastic group movements which reinforce our belief that we really are committed to the following of Jesus; the more sophisticated version of this move is to seek help from the zeitgeist, reading the gospels in the light of the last issue of *Psychology Today*, proving to ourselves that we really are OK and that our discomfort is merely a matter of conditioning. In either case we are looking toward the preservation of the self we are asked to leave behind. We can't believe that "sell all you have, give it to the poor, and follow me," really means "sell all you have, give it to the poor, and follow me." Here we fall back on Kant's ethical imperative and ask (knowing that there is no real danger of this happening), "What would happen if everyone did that?" But the statement is not addressed to everyone, only to you. That fact is one we fall all over ourselves to avoid.

The response we should make to this impasse is to take some encouragement from the answer of Jesus to his apostles when they asked, in response to his hard sayings, "Who then can be saved?" He answered that what was impossible for man was possible because of God's mercy. Some of our dilemma was described by Paul, when he said "the good I would do, I do not." We believe that we are baptized into Christ's death as well as his resurrection. Our consciousness of failure may be part of the death we are asked to acknowledge. It becomes fatal only when we stop acknowledging it, or try to justify it.

This is one aspect of the confession of sin that often escapes us, because we have made of sin a legal thing, a matter of "committing sins" rather than a matter of the condition in which we ordinarily find ourselves; half-hearted, distracted from what we are, and what we are called to. When Christians stop confessing that they are sinners, unprofitable servants, and to that extent that they are not Christians, then Christian faith ends. Consciousness of sin is in this sense the result of baptism: We are baptized into the death of Christ, who was "made sin for us," as well as his resurrection. Sin is death, and to acknowledge this is the beginning of freedom from death. This means a ruthless honesty, however. You cannot confess sin in the abstract. When John says that the person who denies that he is a sinner is a liar, he does not mean that our response should be an abstract confession of sin but rather an acknowledgement of the sin which is *really* there; and he associates this with the Divine light, which reveals darkness. Kierkegaard defined the best Christian confession as a confession of the fact that we are not Christians.

The problem with the confession of sins, the acknowledgement of the death into which we are

baptized, is that it is meant to lead to life. "Wherever we go we carry death with us in our body, the
death that Jesus died, that in this body also life
may reveal itself, the life that Jesus lives. For con-
tinually, while still alive, we are being surren-
dered into the hands of death, for Jesus' sake, so
that the life of Jesus also may be revealed in this
mortal body of ours" (2 Cor. 4:10-11). The form of
this life is something revealed to us not only in the
person of Jesus, but also in the lives of those who,
like Francis, made deliberate, mad-seeming ef-
forts to break with the world of death. Their foolishness is a measure of how radical the break may
have to be; our instinctive reaction against the
behavior of the fool for Christ is not necessarily a
measure of our sanity, but may be the death-
world's way of fighting back.

Before his conversion, Francis was a pleasant
young man who was known for his cheerfulness
and for his generosity to beggars. When he was
about twenty he was imprisoned with a number of
others who had been caught up in the battle between the cities of Perugia and Assisi. His impris-
onment lasted about a year, and upon his release
Francis became dangerously ill. The illness was
lengthy, and it may have been the beginning of his
conversion. He set out to join the Pope's armies,
having bought expensive equipment and clothing,
but along the way he met a poor man and felt such
compassion for him that he exchanged his own
clothes for the other man's rags. Shortly afterwards Francis became ill once more. Instead of

proceeding to battle, he returned to Assisi, realizing that a change was demanded of him. One day
he encountered a leper and at first he was hor-
rified. But then his horror at the leper turned
around to become a horror at his own revulsion.
He embraced the leper, and from that time onward his life turned toward the radical following
of the gospel message.

This incident is one which seemed pivotal to
Francis himself. In his *Testament* he wrote, "The
Lord God gave me, Francis, this way of doing
penance: I was a sinner and found it hard to look
at lepers, and the Lord God led me among them,
and I was merciful to them. As I left them, what
had previously seemed bitter turned into sweetness of body and soul. And then, soon after, I left
the world." (This quotation, as well as the quotations from the *Fioretti* used in this Chapter, can be
found in *The Little Flowers of St. Francis and
Other Franciscan Writings*, translated by Serge
Hughes, Mentor, 1964.)

Francis began to spend time caring for the ill,
giving what he could to the poor; and then came
the incident which marked him as a fool for Christ.
One day as he prayed in the church of St. Damian
he heard a voice tell him "Repair my house, which
is falling down." With his usual literalness Francis assumed that this meant the church in which
he was praying, so he set about repairing it. Unfortunately, he used some of his father's goods in
the process, selling them and offering the proceeds to the poor priest who lived at the church.

The priest refused the money, which Francis left lying on a window sill. Francis' father was understandably angry. When he finally caught Francis (who had retreated for prayer and fasting, and possibly to avoid his father) he took him home forcefully, and kept him locked up there. Francis escaped, returning to St. Damian's, where his father angrily confronted him with a choice: return home or renounce his inheritance, and return the stolen goods. Francis told his father that he was willing to lose his inheritance, but he insisted that the money received from the sale of his father's goods belonged to the poor. Francis' father tried to take him to court; Francis refused the authority of a civil tribunal. The Bishop of Assisi therefore became the judge. He told Franics that he should return what he had taken from his father. Francis agreed, and saying, "These clothes also belong to him," he stripped himself naked. He repudiated his father, telling him, "Until now I have called you my father on earth; now I say, 'Our Father, who art in Heaven.'" His father went home, angry and extremely distressed, and Francis was given the tunic of a laborer who worked for the bishop. From that day he was in every way "the poor man of Assisi," who depended only on God and the charity of others.

Legend should not blind us to what happened here. Francis' treatment of his father was not fair, in any sense of the word. He had in fact stolen his father's property, he tried to refuse restitution, and his repudiation of his father seems self-dramatizing and insensitive. Forgetting that it is St. Francis who did these things, we would be inclined to say of a person who behaved this way that he was mad, ungrateful, disrespectful, and unkind.

Singing the praises of God, Francis left the bishop and accepted a life which included abject poverty, beatings, and the ridicule of those who could see only foolishness in his repudiation of his family and his odd habit of repairing churches. He lived by begging. He also began to try to live a literal interpretation of the words of the gospel, so that when he heard "Provide no gold, silver, or copper to fill your purse, no pack for the road, no second coat, no shoes, no stick," he gave away the few clothes he had begged from others and kept only one shabby coat, which he tied with a rope.

Gradually, the abuse of the townspeople turned to admiration. Francis' charity to the sick and the deformed proved that there was more than eccentricity at work in his life. There were rumors of cures performed by Francis, and a community began to form around Francis. Men from the region were led by his example to undertake the same life. They joined him, leaving their former comfortable lives for a life of poverty and manual labor; where work could not be found, they were told to "have recourse to the table of the Lord"— which is to say, they were to beg. In his Testament, Francis insists upon poverty: "Let the brothers see to it that they do not receive, on any

account, churches and houses made for them, if
these are not in keeping with holy poverty . . . let
them always adhere to these injunctions and live
in the world like strangers and pilgrims."

Francis' view of poverty was absolute, and so
was his view of self-discipline. He threw himself
into a thorn bush when troubled by temptation; he
fasted frequently; he insisted upon obedience but
at the same time was willing to be rebuked by his
followers—in fact he frequently demanded it.
When the order had become established and
somewhat respectable, Francis fought unsuccess-
fully to keep it from becoming attached to property. Many of the friars had come to feel that the
absolute poverty and the unproscribed asceticism
advocated by Francis should be placed within a
more secure framework, one which could include
ownership of land and a regulated form of self-
denial. Francis was enraged. "My brothers," he
said, "the Lord has called me to the way of simplicity and humbleness, and this is the way He has
pointed out to me for myself and for those who will
believe and follow me. The Lord told me that he
would have me poor and foolish in this world, and
that he willed not to lead us by any way other than
by that. May God confound you by your own
wisdom and learning and, for all your fault-
finding, send you back to your vocation whether
you will or not." When some members of the order
wanted to receive official church recognition for
their preaching, in the form of a license from the
Pope to preach in every diocese, Francis said that

they should live lives which by their holiness
would lead bishops to ask the friars for their help.
"Let it be your unique privilege to have no privilege," he said.

He did nothing by halves. The *Fioretti* says that
when Brother Ruffino did not obey him instantly,
Francis, to chastise him, ordered him to preach
naked to the people in Assisi. Then, when Ruffino
had left, Francis was angry with himself for the
harshness of his order and so he too went naked to
Assisi, to join Ruffino. The people who saw them
assumed that they were mad, until they listened to
the words of Francis, who "spoke so marvelously
of the contempt of the world, of holy penance, of
voluntary poverty, of the desire of the heavenly
kingdom, and of the nakedness and humiliation of
the passion of our Lord Jesus Christ, that all those
present, a great number of men and women,
began to weep aloud with great devotion."

What can we make of this extreme behavior, of
a man who takes such abrupt leave of his family
and refuses to compromise at any point? His
father had reason to be angry with him; his friars
later found his way of life too demanding, and
their desire for some security was certainly reasonable. His behavior was always a bit wild.

First of all, it should be said that the age was in
need of a shock. The church was decadent in the
extreme. During the late 12th and early 13th
centuries, the time of Francis' life, the Cathar
church was making converts—largely because of
the corruption of the established church. The

Cathars were dualists, who believed that the world was the creation of a fallen spirit; to be freed from the demonic spirit which ruled the world, to free the Divine light imprisoned in the flesh, severe asceticism was necessary. The Cathar *perfecti*—the closest thing to a Cathar clergy—received a sacrament called the *Consolamentum* following which they were not allowed to marry, or eat meat. Their fasts were extreme. Their poverty was exemplary—so much that the poverty of the Dominican friars, whose order was founded to combat the Cathars, had more to do with countering the powerful Cathar influence than with evangelical poverty. The Cathars combined their ascetic living and voluntary poverty with a compassion for all life, and their kindness to animals was considered unusual. Their teachings were widely accepted in the south of France and the north of Italy, though few Cathar believers felt able to accept the rigors of the life demanded of the *perfecti*. Cathar doctrine was frequently spread by two odd groups of travelers: troubador poets, and weavers.

Although his Catholicism isn't in question—he insisted on his absolute acceptance of Church teaching—Francis' way of life was, in the opinion of many scholars, influenced by Cathar thought. His radical poverty, his extreme asceticism, his feeling for animals, his poetry, his pacifism (he forbade the lay people who joined his third order to carry arms for any purpose)—all of these were closer to Cathar thinking than to the conventional

Catholic thought of Francis' day. How direct the influence was is impossible to determine, and it is probably best to say that Francis and the Cathars responded to the same set of problems, though Francis' response was a kind of unorthodox orthodoxy, where the Cathars (more rule-bound than Francis ever was) were orthodox heretics. In any case, it took a radical effort to understand the gospel clearly in a time when the church was both established and decadent. Francis' movement served as a reforming influence, and some have gone so far as to say that if it had been more successful there would never have been a reformation (though the rise of nationalism and consequent anti-Roman feelings make this doubtful).

But his major purpose was not reform. Francis simply tried to live what he heard in the gospel, and the simplicity and whole-heartedness of the attempt made him appear foolish.

It is hard, in any terms that we can understand, to see all of his actions sympathetically. It is better to see in them the literal application of such gospel counsels as "If anyone comes to me and does not hate his father and mother, wife and children, brothers and sisters, even his own life, he cannot be a disciple of mine. No one who does not carry his cross and come with me can be a disciple of mine." This demand for singlemindedness and total surrender to God led to Francis' repudiation of his father, his obsession with Jesus' passion, and his definition of obedience: It meant, he said, that you should be like a dead body. Before words like those of Jesus, and lives like those of Francis, we are uncomfortable. Rather than offer a defense of the words it is important to see the fruits of trying to live them, something the gospel shows us in the resurrection and the joy of Pentecost, and the lives of saints show us by revealing a little of the kingdom of God. In Francis' case we find tales of the kingdom in the *Fioretti*, a collection of Franciscan stories which was compiled within a couple of generations of Francis' death. The spirit which informs the *Fioretti* is the spirit of poverty— what it means to leave absolutely everything for the sake of the kingdom of God. The impression is one of sustained ecstasy, and it is sometimes frightening:

"St. Francis went behind the altar and began to pray. In that prayer he received a divine visitation that inflamed his soul with such love of holy poverty that from the color of his face and the frequent opening of his mouth it seemed as if flames of fire came from him. Coming towards his companion as if aflame he cried out, 'Ah, ah, ah! Brother Masseo, come to me!' He repeated this three times, and the third time lifted Brother Masseo into the air with his very breath, and propelled him the distance one could hurl a spear. Brother Masseo . . . later told his companions that when he had been raised by the Saint's breath and so softly thrown, he had felt such sweetness of soul and consolation of the Holy Spirit as he had never felt before or since."

Stories like this one remind us of something so simple we tend to forget it: God is much stronger than we think. I am reminded of a story repeated by Elie Wiesel in *Souls on Fire* (Random House, 1972) about the son of the Baal Shem who asked his dead father in a dream, "'How can I serve God?' The Baal Shem climbed a high mountain and threw himself into the abyss. 'Like this,' he answered. Another time the Baal Shem appeared to him as a mountain on fire, erupting into a thousand flaming fragments: 'And like this as well.'" Wiesel relates another story, one close to the story of Brother Masseo: "'One day,'" Rebbe Wolfe of Zhitomir tells us, 'we were all sitting around the table in the House of Study. It was a Friday afternoon. We could hear the Maggid, in his study next door, reading the Sidra, the weekly portion of Scripture customarily read on Shabbat. Suddenly he stopped, the door opened, and there he was, standing motionless in the doorway, staring at us, or perhaps at someone beyond us. His whole being was on fire, but most of all, his face, most of all, his eyes. Seized with panic, Rebbe Pinhas, Rebbe Shmelke, Rebbe Elimelekh and Rebbe Zusia ran into the street. Rebbe Levi-Yitzhak hid under the table. As for me, gripped by a strange exultation, I began to applaud with all my strength—and to this day I regret it.'"

These stories come from the Hasidic tradition, a Jewish movement which has much in common with Franciscanism, including tales of conversion, enthusiasm, asceticism, and ecstasy. They remind us that God is not an idea, a static being towards whom we aspire, but instead is a fire. From the burning bush, God gave his name to Moses: I Am. And that Being was not a metaphysical notion but a fire which burns without consuming. That fire led to the ecstasy known by one of Francis' first followers, Brother Giovanni, who was so given over to God that "at times when he would hear his Master speak of God, his heart would melt like wax near a fire; and the love of God so inflamed him that he was not able to stand still and endure it. He would get up and, as if drunk in spirit, would go about now through the garden, now through the woods, now through the church, talking as the flame and the impetus of the spirit moved him." Brother Masseo, after a period of torment, was given such a joyful humility that "frequently when in prayer he would make a steady jubilant sound, like a soft dove. . . . When asked by Brother Jacopo de Fallerone why he never changed the tone of his rejoicing, he answered with great joy that when something goes well there is no need to change it."

The ecstatic element of Franciscan spirituality is balanced by a deep sense of compassion and mercy. One young friar, on seeing that a criminal had been sentenced by a harsh mayor to have his eyes put out, "asked that one eye be taken from him and the other from the evildoer, so that the criminal would not be completely deprived of his sight. The mayor and the council, seeing the fervent charity of the friar, pardoned both him and the criminal.''

The Franciscan approach to life takes us to what we would normally regard as extremes: extremes of charity, of asceticism, of ecstasy, and certainly extremes of behavior. The madness involved in being a fool for Christ could have to do with the words of scripture: that no one can look upon the face of God and live. There is a story told by the Hasidim about four men who made their way into the presence of God. One upon seeing God went mad, another died, another lost his faith, and only one survived intact. A clear sense of God could so unmoor a person from ordinary allegiances, ordinary behavior, that he might seem genuinely insane to us. But the insanity of a Francis is more sane than our caution, and his concentration on the death of Christ is more life-giving than our pursuit of self-fulfillment. The medieval fascination with Jesus' suffering has been criticized by a number of commentators, who point out that where eastern Christianity emphasizes the transfiguration, western Christians emphasize the stigmata and the passion.

Finally it is all one: The Russian Church, with its transfigured saints, saw a great mystery in the humiliated Christ. Our culture is puritanical about suffering, and forgets that it is not a Christian obsession but a permanent reality. It is the beginning of Buddha's revelation, and Plato said that the love of wisdom meant learning how to die. Francis received the stigmata, but the resurrection and the transfiguration are there. The *Fioretti* speaks of Francis transfigured, so that "his five stigmata were as five beautiful stars and so radiant that they lit the entire palace with their rays." Reading the *Fioretti*—especially at points like this one—we feel a certain embarrassment, as if we had outgrown that kind of story. But learning to read that kind of story "with eyes that can see" might be the most important task for modern Christians, who should not be embarrassed by this any more than they are by the miracle of loaves and fishes multiplied, or water changed to wine. We can be refreshed in all of this attempt at coming to renewed understandings by the life of Francis. But it is also a challenge to the lukewarmness we are accustomed to, a lukewarmness which without his life, and the lives of others who have tried to understand the gospel radically and wholeheartedly, would be reinforced without a challenge on any side.

Chapter Two

Mary

There seems to be a great gulf between the Mary we encounter in scripture and the one presented to us by later church tradition. Except for the opening chapters of Luke's gospel, the New Testament has little to say about her. She is mentioned only a few times once the stories of Jesus' birth and youth are over, and there is nothing in the scripture about Mary, the queen of heaven. But this exalted idea of Mary became a firm part of Christian thought before too many years had passed. Although the Reformation brought an end to devotion to Mary among many Christians, the original intention of the greatest reformers was to purify a devotion which had become overladen with superstition. Martin Luther, for example, wrote, "The 'great things' are nothing less than that she became the mother of God, in which work so many and such great good things are bestowed on her as pass man's understanding. For on this there follows all honor, all blessedness, and her unique place in the whole of mankind, among which she has no equal. . . . It needs to be pondered in the heart what it means to be the Mother of God." Calvin, in protesting abuses of devotion to Mary wrote, "We truly do not want to take in the least from the honor which is her due, but nothing is withheld from her by not making her into a goddess. On the contrary people do Mary a great disservice when they disfigure her with false praise and rob God of what belongs to him." Calvin recommended the imitation of Mary: "We must not just praise her in word, we must follow her example. The greatest praise we can offer is when we recognize her as our teacher and become her pupils. . . . Realizing that God in his grace has looked on her, we wish to see in her, as in a mirror, the mercy of God." (The quotations from Luther and Calvin are both taken from *In Praise of Mary,* by Donal Flanagan, Veritas Publications, Dublin, 1975).

The attitude of the reformers later developed into one of opposition to any Marian devotion; this became, along with other aspects of the cult of the saints, a casualty of the Reformation and Counter-reformation. The casualty worked both ways: Protestants lost what they might have gained from a renewed appreciation of Mary, one salvaged from centuries of superstition, and Catholics were presented with a distorted picture of Mary—the distortions were maintained more firmly than ever because they were under attack. It is an old maxim that we become what our enemies make us. Following the Reformation, Catholics became more insistent than ever about the doctrines of the real presence of Christ in the Eucharist, devotion to Mary, and the authority of the church, precisely because those doctrines had come under heavy fire. And if Catholics became more papist than ever before, Protestants, in response to Rome's counter-offensive, became more-Protestant-than-thou, vying with each other to see who could strip away as many remnants of the old faith as possible.

The respect which Christians have shown for each other in recent years—a respect which is based on the understanding that Baptism is a sacrament which transcends denominational lines—has allowed Catholics to see that many of the Reformation charges were justified. Occasionally we were presented with a picture of Mary which is simply unreconcilable with the God revealed to us in Jesus: She was to be the mediator between us and Jesus, according to some Marian extremists, and we were sometimes given the notion that Mary periodically had to soothe a wrathful, violent God (more like a pirate king than a loving Father). This picture is happily gone forever.

Among Protestants there is similarly a realization that too much could have been jettisoned with the Reformation, as fundamentally necessary as it may have been. This is shown by the new emphasis on liturgy in many Protestant churches, with a consequent appreciation of the sacramental activity of the church.

Is it possible—given the relatively scarce mention of her in scripture—to come to an understanding of Mary which can speak to us in contemporary terms? I think we can approach Mary best by understanding the way in which she exemplified the paradox of the kingdom which God revealed in Jesus. In Matthew's gospel Jesus' teaching opens with a set of paradoxes. We have domesticated them, referring easily to "the Beatitudes," that is to say "the Blesseds"—and although this shorthand is helpful, sometimes we forget who Jesus calls blessed. They are those the world tends to consider anything *but* blessed: those who mourn, those who are meek, those who make peace and are whole-hearted (we know how easily they are taken in), those who are persecuted, those who are poor. This teaching, of course, did not come for the first time with Jesus. It was the constantly repeated message of the prophets, who made it clear that it was mercy and justice, not mere observance of the law, which were signs of faith. In Jesus it is given new intensity, elevated to absolute heights. He tells his followers that they are not only forbidden to murder—they must not even be angry. On point after point he moves from exterior observance of the law to absolute interior acceptance of its spirit—the passage is from just dealings with all men, even your enemies, to the impossible demand that we love our enemies; and we are to do this because God does it. "You are to be perfect, as your Father in heaven is perfect." If this is possible, then the kingdom *must* be at hand: It upsets everything.

The upsetting nature of the gospel was celebrated by Mary. Her praise of God in Luke's gospel reads like one of the psalms: "His name is Holy; his mercy sure from generation to generation towards those who fear him:/the deeds his own right arm has done disclose his might:/the arrogant of heart he has put to rout,/he has brought down monarchs from their thrones,/but the humble have been lifted high./The hungry he has satisfied with good things,/the rich sent empty away" (Luke 1: 49-53).

These world-upsetting things were understood to be signs of the arrival of God's reign. When the disciples of John the Baptist brought John's question to Jesus—"Are you the one who is to come?"—Jesus answered, "Go and tell John what you hear and see: The blind recover their sight, the lame walk, the lepers are made clean, the deaf hear, the dead are raised to life, the poor are hearing the good news" (Matthew 11, 3-5). All of these things are signs that a new energy has broken through into the world—the power of God, making all things new. It is interesting that the fact of good news for the poor is considered as miraculous as the raising of the dead or the healing of the ill; but this is again very much in the prophetic tradition: The way of the Lord is paved by justice. This sense is carried through in Jesus' command that his followers, if they wished to be perfect, should sell everything and give it to the poor, and in his parable of the final judgement it is compassion for the downtrodden, not piety, which is the basis of God's judgement: Whatever is done to the least human being is done to God.

But the energy which accomplishes these things is not the sort which begins with political intrigues or force of arms. It comes rather from the recognition of God's will for us, the obedience which allows his work to be done. This is what Luther means when he says that "we must ponder what it means to be the mother of God," and Calvin means when he says that we must "recognize her as our teacher and become her pupils".

Kierkegaard used the contrast between the Mary of the sentimentalists and the Mary of scripture to show her true importance. "What they leave out," he wrote, "is the distress, the dread, the paradox. . . . To be sure, Mary bore the child miraculously, but it came to pass with her after the manner of women, and that season is one of dread, distress, and paradox. To be sure, the angel was a ministering spirit, but it was not a servile spirit which obliged her by saying to the other young maidens of Israel, 'Despise not Mary. What befalls her is the extraordinary.' But the angel came only to Mary, and no one could understand her. After all, what woman was so mortified as Mary? And is it not true in this instance also that one whom God blesses He curses in the same breath? This is the spirit's interpretation of Mary, and she is not (as it shocks me to say, but shocks me still more to think that they have thoughtlessly and coquettishly interpreted her thus)—she is not a fine lady who sits in state and plays with an infant god. Nevertheless, when she says 'Behold the handmaid of the Lord'—then she is great, and I think it will not be found difficult to explain why she became the Mother of God. She has no need of worldly admiration, any more than Abraham has need of tears, for she was not a heroine, and he was not a hero, but both of them became greater than such, not at all because they were exempted from distress and torment and paradox, but they became great through these" (*Fear and Trembling,* tr. by Walter Lowrie, Anchor Books, pp 75-76).

Kierkegaard compares Mary to Abraham. They are alike, in that both faced a God they had known as a God of mercy and justice, a God who kept faith with man, and suddenly the demand of that God was terrifying, and the terror had to be endured in total isolation. God asks Abraham to do something abhorrent: No one in the world is so loathed as the man who would kill his child. Mary is asked to bear a child without a husband, to be a pregnant woman whose baby comes from God—absurd, a claim every society would ridicule. (A similar faith is asked of Joseph—he is asked to believe that Mary's absurd claim is true. He must sometimes have asked himself if he didn't perhaps imagine the angel, if he was not in fact a fool.)

We have lived with the story so long that we miss what Kierkegaard calls our attention to: the distress, the dread, the paradox. We have celebrated Christmas over and over again, domesticating the story of a God whose demands can seem wild and terrible. What was demanded of Mary has to do with the mystery of evil—that is, the mystery not of willed evil, the evil human perversity accomplishes, but rather the radical evil

present in all human suffering, the suffering of the
innocent which seems so fruitless and so unfair.

Leon Bloy wrote, "A woman saint may fall into
the mire and a prostitute may ascend into light,
but never will either of them be able to become a
respectable woman" (Pilgrim of the Absolute,
Eyre and Spottiswoode, p. 307). Mary must have
endured a certain amount of ridicule from "respectable people" all of her life. Our own society
stigmatizes women who have children outside of
marriage. We should realize that this is precisely
the way Mary must have appeared to her contemporaries—as a foolish woman with a gullible
cuckold for a husband and a disturber of the
peace for a son. It was among people like this that
God chose to come.

God chose to take what the world ridicules and
despises, the world of respectable people and the
institutions which support their sense of their own
righteousness, and make it the vehicle of his son's
entry into the life of the world. This is an uncomfortable picture of Mary, and we would rather
drag her into the world we prefer, the world of
respectability, in which we worship a predictable
God who could never make us uncomfortable.

With characteristic irony, Kierkegaard says, "I
think it will not be found difficult to explain why
she became the Mother of God." In a terrible
sense it is very simple: It is because she could say,
and mean it, "Be it done according to your will." It
was because she was able to say this that the
Word became flesh in her. Despite the dread,

the risk, the strangeness of the God she faced
directly for the first time, she was able to accept
the will of God completely and God was free to act.
The incredible truth is that a human being was as
necessary to the work of redemption as God is—it
could not have happened without her cooperation.
People have talked frequently of Mary's humility,
and of course humility is required to make the
response Mary made. But the real humility is the
humility of a God who waits for the cooperation of
human beings before he acts, who asks us to be
part of the dialectic from which the new creation
comes.

It is as a model of faith, of what faith means,
that Mary can matter to us now. In order for the
Word to become flesh in each of us, we have to be
prepared to meet a God as strange as the one
Mary met, and this means prayer and attention.
We have to open ourselves and become whole-
hearted, so that it can be possible for us to say,
"Be it done as you will." That response can't be
faked. And it is a necessary one—necessary not
only to our own salvation but also to the work
which God wants to do.

Simeon told Mary in the temple that Jesus was
"a sign which men reject; and you too shall be
pierced to the heart. Many in Israel will stand or
fall because of him, and thus the secret thoughts
of many will be laid bare" (Luke 2: 34-35). Mary
was called on to share in the suffering of God, and
therefore in the work of revealing "the secret
thoughts of many hearts," the uncovering of the

truth which was the work of the prophets and of Jesus, and which is—strange as it seems—our work as well. It is true that scripture says little about her, but this may be in order to emphasize the moment that made her great, the moment that finally is what being a saint is about: She was able, once, to say "Be it done, as you will," and that changed everything.

Chapter Three

Thomas More

Samuel Johnson called him "the person of the greatest virtue these islands ever produced." Despite the four centuries which separate our time from his, Thomas More strikes us as a thoroughly modern man. He was not martyred for reasons which were blindingly clear, even to him. His martyrdom was not at all like that of Ignatius or Justin Martyr, and he seems to have had doubts about the stand he took. Although he was resigned to it, he certainly did not want to die; but he went to his death, for reasons of conscience, because he knew that to do otherwise would be a betrayal. To stay alive would mean swearing an oath which he believed to be false.

In introducing his play about More, *A Man for all Seasons*, Robert Bolt writes, "I am not a Catholic or even in the meaningful sense of the word a Christian. So by what right do I appropriate a Christian saint to my purposes? Or to put it another way, why do I take as my hero a man who brings about his own death because he can't put his hand on an old black book and tell an ordinary lie?" Because, Bolt writes, More was "a hero of self-hood" (*A Man for All Seasons*, by Robert Bolt, Heinemann, 1960). He was more than that, but he was *at least* that, which has made him a hero not only for Christians but for those who are able to recognize nobility in any form.

We are lucky in having a full picture of More. The problem in dealing with most saints (or for that matter with most figures from history) is that we have the bare facts and little else, just a record of what they did and sometimes a record of what they might have said on some important occasion. The thinness with which historical figures usually come across to us is a sign of how little we have when we have only the facts; so a man like Alexander the Great, who really existed, seems less real to us than a man like Odysseus, who did not. Thanks to his friend Erasmus and his son-in-law Roper, More is as real as any character from fiction.

Thomas More, the son of a judge, followed his father in the study of law. (His father must have had mixed feelings about his son's facility at legal argument: Once when Thomas successfully argued against a claim of the king's, the king responded by putting Thomas' father in jail.) He was later appointed a judge himself, and throughout his career was known for fairness and impartiality.

He was also known for his learning. His interests ranged widely, from theology to animal behavior (he kept a menagerie, and his pet monkey is immortalized in Holbein's portrait of the More family). He was known to be a brilliant thinker, but his fame increased with the continental publication of *Utopia*, and it was curiosity about More which led Erasmus to send Ulrich von Hutten the word portrait we have of him. It is a wonderful

picture: More, Erasmus says, is "the most delightful character in the world. . . . He seems to be
born and made for friendship, of which he is the
sincerest and most persistent devotee. . . . While
he is somewhat neglectful of his own interest, no
one takes more pains in attending to the concerns
of his friends. What more need I say? If anyone
asks for a perfect example of true friendship, it is
in More that he will best find it. In company, his
extraordinary kindness and sweetness of temper
are such as to cheer the dullest spirit. . . . From
boyhood he was always so pleased with a joke that
it might seem that jesting was the main object of
his life. . . . No one is less swayed by the opinion of
the multitude, but on the other hand no one sticks
more closely to common sense." (This, and the
quotations from *Roper's Life of Thomas More*, as
well as the quotations from More's letters, are
taken from *The Utopia of Thomas More, including
Roper's Life of More and Letters of More and his
Daughter Margaret*, D. Van Nostrand Co., 1947.)
Erasmus describes More physically and tells us of
his personal habits—he was inclined to simplicity
and disliked ornament, liked his food plain but did
not "shrink from things that impart an innocent
pleasure, even of a bodily kind, and has always a
good appetitie for milk-puddings and for fruit, and
eats a dish of eggs with the greatest relish."
Throughout his account of More's character two
things stand out: More must have been one of the
most attractive human beings imaginable, and one
of the most virtuous.

This is rare. Most saints, like most people, have quirks of one sort or another which we have to see through, if we want to appreciate them. If there is a charity and dedicated love which shines in Catherine of Siena, it shines through a personality which also went in for extremes of asceticism, extremes which were so severe that they killed her at a fairly young age. Francis of Assisi is undoubtedly heroic, and his following of Christ is attractive—as long as we place a distance between ourselves and Francis, and ignore the fact that if his sort of person were to appear in contemporary times he could easily repel us, since he would certainly seem to be an uncompromising fanatic.

In Thomas More we find something different. He was ascetic, but in a rather mild way. Roper tells us "albeit he appeared honorable outwardly, and like one of his calling, yet inwardly, no such vanities esteeming, he secretly wore next to his body a shirt of hair which my sister More, a young gentlewoman, chancing to espy as he sat in the summer alone in his doublet and hose, wearing thereon a plain shirt without ruff or collar, began to laugh at it. My wife, not ignorant of his habit, perceiving the same privately told him of it, and he being sorry that she saw it, presently amended it. . . ." Hairshirts, uncomfortable as they were, were not an uncommon thing for pious Christians in More's time. More made sure that his family gathered daily for prayer; he reminded them of their religious obligations frequently, and he set aside

Fridays for prayer in a place he built away from his house for solitude. He was good to the poor in his village of Chelsea. When he heard that a woman in the village was in labor he prayed until someone brought him news of the successful delivery of the child. He sang in his church choir, despite the protests of his friend the Duke of Norfolk: "God body, God body, my lord Chancellor, a parish clerk, a parish clerk, you dishonor the King and his office!"

More's piety was of a balanced and attractive sort. As a young man he had given some thought to becoming a Carthusian monk, and spent some time living with the order (as young laymen often did in those times, lodging with monks while they pursued their studies), but, Erasmus says, "he could not shake off his wish to marry. Accordingly he resolved to be a chaste husband rather than a licentious priest." He married twice, first Jane Colt, who was seventeen when she married More and died at the age of twenty-six, leaving four children: Margaret, Elizabeth, Cecily, and John. More married a second time soon after Jane's death, and this time he chose a widow, Alice Middleton, with whom he had no child, though she brought her child—also named Alice—into the More household. More was unusual for his time in that he believed in the education of women. He taught his wives music, and his daughters were more learned in the classics than most men of the day.

More's honesty, his personal attractiveness, his

wit, his ability as a judge, all combined to make
him interesting to Henry VIII. More was, according to Erasmus, not so attracted to the court as the
court was attracted to him: "He was rather dis-
inclined to Court life and to any intimacy with
princes, having always a special hatred of tyranny
and a great fancy for equality." Why did More
join Henry's court, then? Because it was not like
other courts, Erasmus says, and More apparently
agreed with him. Henry was intelligent, zealous in
the defense of the Catholic faith against Lutheran
heresy, and witty as well—three qualities which
were not found too frequently in kings, and qualities which made him in some ways a man after
More's heart. In some ways—because More saw,
as people around him did not, how dangerous
Henry's ambition was, and how lightly he wore the
obligations of friendship. Once, when Henry made
a special trip to More's house to see him and
walked in More's garden with his arm around
More's shoulders, Roper was delighted. Wasn't
More pleased, Roper asked, that he should be
such an intimate friend of the King? More replied,
"I thank our Lord, son. I find his Grace my very
good Lord indeed, and I do believe he does as
singularly favor me as any subject within his
realm. Howbeit, son Roper, I may tell thee, I have
no cause to be proud thereof. For if my head would
win him a castle in France, it should not fail to
go." Later, after his disagreements with Henry led
More to resign his offices, he told Thomas Cromwell, a new favorite of the King's: "Mr. Cromwell,

you are now entered into the service of a most noble, wise, and liberal prince; if you will follow my poor advice you will, in giving council to his Grace, ever tell him what he ought to do, but never tell him what he is able to do; so shall you show yourself a true faithful servant, and a right worthy Councilor. For if the lion knew his own strength, hard were it for any man to rule him."

What were the events which led More to his death, and how did his friend Henry come to turn so easily on a man for whom he had such clear affection? Henry had, with a dispensation from ordinary canon law, married the widow of his brother Arthur, the Spanish princess Catherine. The marriage was pleasant enough, for some of its course, but then Henry came upon two complications: He had no male heir, and he had fallen in love with Ann Boleyn. In addition, the Spanish alliance which had been cemented by the marriage of Catherine and Henry was no longer as advantageous to England as it had been. The Pope was approached with a request for an annulment of the marriage. Spain had greater influence in Rome than England had at that time, and Henry's sudden scruples over his marriage looked suspicious, following the suspension of ordinary canonical rules which had allowed Henry's marriage in the first place. It is easy to see why the Pope turned Henry's request down.

Henry was irritated. His anger at the Pope coincided with a rise in nationalistic feeling which had spread throughout Europe, and for centuries

theologians whose sympathies were not inclined to
Rome had suggested that the Pope was one bishop
among many. Henry found sympathy for his position among English churchmen. Bishop Thomas
Cranmer was willing to grant his annulment without consulting Rome, and the break with Rome
was sealed.

Henry asked his subjects to swear an oath of
agreement to the statement that the King of England was supreme head on earth of the church in
England. Thomas More had hoped it would not
come to that. He had never denied the right of
parliament to legislate in such matters as the marriage of the king, and indeed he offered in his own
defense the fact that once, when Henry had been
strongly pro-Pope, More had urged him to moder-
ate his defense of the Pope's authority, which,
More said, should be "more lightly touched," considering that the Pope "is a prince as you are, and
in league with other Christian princes." More
must later have enjoyed the irony of Henry's response, which—he told his accusers—was that
"we are so much bounden unto the See of Rome
that we cannot do too much honor to it."

More's problem was delicate. He simply could
not swear to the oath in the form it had been
offered. He hoped that his peers would accept his
silence as consent, the ordinary legal interpretation of silence in such cases. He refused to tell
his friends or family precisely what his objections
to the oath were, since taking them into his confidence might implicate them, making them legally

culpable—co-conspirators with him in treason. More was willing to swear to his loyalty, to the rights of the English church, to his refusal of all treasonous intention; he was not willing to name Henry supreme head of the church in England, and it was that point which irritated Henry. With relatively few exceptions—none of them of More's stature—every prominent man in England had been willing to sign the oath. More's refusal, backed up by his clever use of the law, stood in sharp contrast to every act of compliance. The need to break him was no longer merely a matter of satisfying Henry's pride. It would be seen as necessary by those who did not, in Bolt's words, find it hard to swear to "an ordinary lie". And of course for many of them it was not really a lie but a convenient gesture. It was not as if the point were all that clear; More himself said that he would be happy to be given an honorable way out. He would not, however, swear an oath which he believed false. His refusal on this point, prolonged as it was, was proving an embarrassment. Finally, after a long confinement in the Tower of London, More was convicted on the basis of perjured testimony given by Richard Rich, who claimed that More had made treasonous statements to him. On July 6, 1535, More was beheaded.

* * *

When I say that More is a thoroughly modern saint, I mean that he represented several trends which later became part of our religious understanding. One of them is the trend towards a lay understanding of the church. Even now the word "religious" is occasionally used of people whose *profession* is religion, as if we were still bound to the hierarchical categories of the middle ages, in which some are kings, some paupers, some religious—all men and women cemented to their places, which transcend them as individuals. ("The king is dead—long live the king!" The statement makes sense only if the office does, and if in addition the office is something which exists without the person who inhabits it. This understanding, including the belief that some offices are *automatically* religious, has died.) In More's case, religion was not a profession in our rigid sense of the word so much as it was a profession in the root sense: a declaration, a commitment, a focussed and deliberate allegiance. It was also, in his case, a modern form of this commitment in this sense: For the early martyrs, death followed the fact that they fell into the category of Christian. If they could be proved Christian, they were automatically guilty. In More's time Christianity—in purely dogmatic terms—was generally accepted. Martin Luther, the Pope, Henry VIII, and the men who judged More guilty all agreed to those doctrines which were considered criminal by the state in the time of Ignatius and Justin. The disagreements had more to do with doctrinal nuance than with doctrine itself, or with jurisdiction and administrative authority. More died for reasons which were subjective in the extreme. Where an Ignatius would have had no heistation in pointing to heretics, More appealed to the consensus of the church as a whole in refusing to name the King supreme head of the church, but in addition he was careful to refrain from counseling others to join him. Part of his appeal, in fact, was the fact that where he was willing to leave others free in conscience to accept the oath, he asked only the same indulgence. This is far from the fanatic defense of anything like a dogma. In asking his daughter Margaret to accept his silence with regard to his reasons for refusing the oath he was quite firm. "For I doubt not but you well remember that the matters which move my conscience (without declaration whereof I can nothing touch the point), I have sundry times told you that I will disclose them to no man." His lack of certainty was such that it was seen as the vulnerable spot it was, in purely logical terms, by those who had allied themselves with the king. In writing to Margaret of a meeting with representatives of the king, during the time of his confinement in the tower, More says, "My Lord of Canterbury taking hold on what I said, that I condemned not the consciences of them that swore, said to me that it well appeared that I did not take it for a very sure and certain thing that I might not lawfully swear, but rather for a thing uncertain and doubtful. 'But then,' said my Lord, 'you know for a certainty, and a thing without doubt, that you are bound to obey your sovereign Lord your King. And therefore you are bound to leave off the doubts of your unsure conscience in refusing the Oath, and take the sure way in obeying your prince, and swear it.' Now it all was so, that in my own mind methought myself not concluded, yet this argument seemed to me suddenly so subtle, and with such authority coming out of so noble a prelate's mouth, that I could again nothing answer thereto, but only that I thought myself I might not well do so, because in my conscience this was one of the cases in which I was not bound that I should obey my prince, since whatsoever other folk thought in the matter (whose conscience or learning I would not condemn nor take upon me to judge), yet in my conscience the truth seemed on t'other side."

Here we see the terrible simplicity with which More approached his death. All his life he knew that his vocation was to follow the will of God, and at times he expressed a mild regret that he had not followed the monastic way. Despite his worldly success he knew what finally was demanded of him, and when the choice became clear it was a terrible one. I think of what Jesus told his disciples when he sent them out into the world: You are to be as wise as serpents and as innocent as doves. More was both. He had in fact made friends of the Mammon of Iniquity: He was a servant of Henry VIII, and while he believed that this was rightly his loyalty he was fully aware of the sort of man Henry was. When he was forced to choose, the choosing was not easy. It brought him up against his friends and his family, and it was a struggle.

Roper mentions a couple of occasions on which More told him that the struggle was going well, or that it had been concluded successfully. Roper, with an understandable naivety, assumed that More meant his case before the King. He realized later that the struggle More referred to was interior. He made his choice and saw it through in isolation, misunderstood by almost everyone. What appeared to More's opponents as clever evasiveness was really very simple: He wanted to avoid being killed, if this could be done honorably, but if it could not then he would die. They saw this only as irritating independence, arrogance, scrupulosity, defiance—everything but what it was, the thing he had to do to be an honest man. The accounts of his death are almost unbearably moving. As he was led to the Tower again after his condemnation, his daughter Margaret ran to him twice, and Roper says that the moment was "to many of them that were present so lamentable that it made them for very sorrow mourn and weep." In the letter he wrote the day before his martyrdom More wrote to Margaret, "I never liked your manner toward me better than when you kissed me last."

The fact that he died for conscientious reasons, reasons so personal that they were bewildering to many good people, is another aspect of More's modernity; and so is the isolation in which he endured his death. But even while his death (as *chosen* as it seemed to be to some of his contemporaries, as necessary as it was to More's integrity) moves us at a personal level, so much so that this seems the most important lesson it has to teach us, it had another equally important effect on his contemporaries. If it were not for his witness the issue of loyalty which Henry raised might have seemed a small thing. The fact that so good a man as Thomas More was willing to die over an oath proved that something deeper was at stake, and that there are deeper loyalties than loyalties to king and to personal convenience. More's death hit Europe's intellectual community hard. Erasmus, More's friend, wrote, "In More's death I seem to have died myself. We had but one soul between us." Earlier Erasmus had written of Henry VIII that "no one more courteous or less exacting than this Prince could be desired." More's witness showed just how exacting a prince could be.

Which brings us to another point: More was a willing servant of the King. There are some who think that this alone—his complicity in what anarchist writers have called "the social lie"—led to his death. Kenneth Rexroth, in writing about More, says "Christians are slowly coming to realize that their religion, even when considered only a system of social ethics, is utterly incompatible with modern civilization." More's tragedy, Rexroth believes (*With Eye and Ear*, Kenneth Rexroth, Herder & Herder, 1970), is that he was "a saintly man destroyed by the delusion of participation." I am tempted to this view, but there are a couple of absolutely necessary qualifications to be made.

One is that modern civilization, as a demon here, is unfairly chosen. There is no civilization which would have welcomed a man who saw an allegiance higher than the one the state, or the king, claims. More's allegiance was not apparent until it was put to the test. When it was, and when he proved himself faithful, he was seen as a threat. But he would have threatened the emperor, or commissar, or president. It is not "modern civilization" which is a threat, but the more general problem of mixed allegiances.

The other qualification is that it is not simply "the delusion of participation" which killed More. Roper's life shows that he was clear-headed about Henry's potentially lethal ambitions. He was not deluded. By being where he was, by being a participant, he revealed a truth. He showed us the limits of participation; he showed us what you *cannot* do if you want to serve God.

Chapter Four

Peter

"It is not the healthy that need a doctor, but the sick," Jesus said. "I did not come to invite virtuous people, but sinners" (Matt. 9: 12-13). Peter, like every saint, was a sinner—a fool, in fact, at times when a hero (if the gospel story were a more conventional one) would have been clear-headed, brave, and spiritually balanced. Peter misunderstands, reacts with excessive emotion, contradicts himself, and even denies any association with Jesus in order to save his own skin. (Someone once said that Vatican diplomacy began in the courtyard where Peter said three times, "I do not know the fellow.")

Even when he is at his best and his intentions are obviously good, Peter frequently appears to be a blunderer. When Jesus spoke to the disciples about his death, "Peter took him by the arm and began to rebuke him: 'Heaven forbid!' he said. 'No, Lord, this shall never happen to you.' Then Jesus turned and said to Peter, 'Away with you, Satan; you are a stumbling block to me. You think as men think, not as God thinks'" (Matt. 16: 22-23).

Jesus seems to be rebuking Peter here for something perfectly natural: "You think as men think, not as God thinks." How else *should* Peter think? Jesus is asking the impossible—or at least he is asking something we ordinarily think of as an impossibility, namely the ability to think in a divine

69

way. There is a clue here to the Christian vocation, and what the clue points to is expanded in the
following verses: "Jesus then said to his disciples,
'If anyone wishes to be a follower of mine, he must
leave self behind; he must take up his cross and
come with me. Whoever cares for his own safety is
lost; but if a man will let himself be lost for my
sake, he will find his true self. What will a man
gain by winning the whole world, at the cost of his
true self? Or what can he give that will buy that
self back?' " (Matt. 16: 24-26). Even Peter's honest
and understandable fear for his master, his loyal
compassion, is still too much a part of the self
Jesus would have Peter (and all of his followers)
lose, in order to find the true self, which thinks as
God thinks.

For Peter, learning the lesson didn't come
easily—not that it ever does; but in Peter's case
we see a man trying and failing, sometimes failing
spectacularly. One of the best gospel stories is
Peter's run across the water, when Peter, on
seeing Jesus walking on the water, begins to do the
same in faith. He sinks only when he doubts for a
second (or perhaps because for a split second he
believes that the power is his own). Because of
that momentary return to the false self, forgotten
in his initial enthusiasm to be with Jesus, he loses
the true self he was beginning to find.

The mistakes which Peter made—and they are
probably his most prominent characteristic, at
least in the gospels—are instructive. When Jesus
prayed at Gethsemane, in isolated terror, Peter

and James and John slept. Jesus directed his rebuke to Peter: "What! Could none of you stay awake with me one hour? Stay awake, and pray that you may be spared the test. The spirit is willing, but the flesh is weak" (Matthew 26: 40-41). Again there is the implication that Jesus' followers must be prepared to do as he does, to accept what he has accepted; and it is true of Peter, finally. "When you are old," Jesus tells him, "you will stretch out your arms, and a stranger will bind you fast, and carry you where you have no wish to go." Jesus said this, John writes, "to indicate the manner of death by which Peter was to glorify God" (John 21: 18-19).

This idea that Christians are to live the life which Christ himself lived is an uncomfortable one. The usual tendency has been to make the "imitation of Christ" an imitation in the narrowest sense—almost an aping of his gestures, as Jung once said, rather than an acceptance of the substance of his life. Going beyond imitation to sharing in the life and death and rising of Christ involves a radical obedience to God's will, one which takes us beyond the ethical dimension implied by the word "imitation," if we mean by imitation a deliberate corresponding of the rules we live by and the rules Christ lived by. Where Christianity is equated with a set of rules or standards—even the loftiest ones—it is distorted. Those standards will *happen* in the life of the Christian; they will not have to be lived up to, as if *that* were the effort we were to aim at. There is

the constant tendency among church people to
move Christianity into the pleasant realms of respectable behavior, to make it out that the Christian and the good citizen are one and the same.
But the demands of Christianity are really non-
sensical if this is all you are after. Jesus said very
little about ethical matters and when he did, the
way he posed the problems made ethical behavior
seem impossible: To look at a woman lustfully was
the same as committing adultery; to be angry was
not really different from killing; his followers were
to give everything away to the poor, and not look
behind them. And as if that weren't strange
enough, there are all the paradoxes: You find your
life by losing it, you can be a master only if you are
first and foremost a servant, you are forgiven as
you forgive. And on top of this are the strange
assurances: You help to create the kingdom by
looking for it diligently. Ask and you shall receive;
knock and it shall be opened; the Holy Spirit will
not be withheld from anyone who asks.

Now the point that makes most Christians aw-
fully uncomfortable is the fact that apart from
these paradoxes and puzzling statements there is
really nothing unique about Christianity. Everything we regard as Christian ethics can be found
in the Old Testament, and in the Greek stoics. The
radical humility, self-denial, and obedience of the
gospels cannot be lived as other ethical systems
can be, by a kind of imitation or deliberate corre-
spondence. Most systems of ethics assume that the
person interested in living up to the code—what-

ever it happens to be—has it within his power to begin from wherever he is and move himself toward the ideal. But Christianity begins with the confession of sinfulness. After hours and hours of fruitless fishing, Jesus fills Peter's net and his response is to say, "Leave me, Lord, sinner that I am." This response is made not so much because Peter senses what a terrible human being he is, but rather because he had had a glimpse of God's generosity, and a consequent awe leaves him feeling unworthy. It is not the neurotic grovelling which enjoys the feeling of abasement but the honest sense of infinite smallness which comes to those who have seen real glory.

The revelation of human sinfulness makes sense only when seen in this light, the light of the incomprehensible goodness of God. It is not meant to dwarf human beings but to raise them up—because it is shared. Simone Weil called the relationships "algebraic": In several places she pointed out the equation you can find in statements like "As the Father sent me, so I send you," and "Love one another as I have loved you." The paradox is that it is only by realizing his ungratefulness that a man can begin to be grateful. It is only by confessing his sins that a man can escape from being bound by them. And it is only by acknowledging the fact that God alone is the giver of life, that by himself he is nothing, that man can begin to share in the life of God himself, and become what Jesus is.

This paradoxical nature of Christianity may be

why Jesus chose Peter to be the leader of the early church. He could not have found a man more full of human failing than Peter, a man who after protesting his loyalty denies Jesus three times. But Jesus asks him, three times, "Do you love me?" And it is in this context that Jesus tells him, "Feed my sheep," linking Peter's love for Jesus with his leadership. Peter's virtue, unlike the virtue of the classical hero, is absurd: He falls and rises, falls and rises, never quite striking the final noble pose. But there is a great difference between the Peter of the gospels and the Peter of the Acts of the Apostles. The Peter we see in the Acts of the Apostles is not without faults, but they are not the old ones. When he is too strict in his application of the Jewish proscription against eating with Gentiles, he is shown that he is wrong, and changes accordingly. When Paul opposes him—even hints that he is guilty of moral cowardice—over Peter's strict observance of Jewish law, Peter accepts the correction. Peter's leadership is secure enough to allow him to be seen as weak; it allows him to be wrong. It also allows him to listen, to his fellow Christians and to God. Peter's prayer and attention allowed him to receive God's message, the message that Gentiles too are to be included in the fullness of God's revelation, that Gentiles too will receive the Holy Spirit. When the Gentile Cornelius and Peter, the Jew, were led to each other in prayer, something of permanent importance happened in history, but it happened because of a willingness on Peter's part to wait, listen, and pray.

Peter was leader *within* the church, not *over* it. This may be the difference between church authority, as it ought to be (and is not, very frequently), and secular authority (which is too frequently imitated by church authority). Jesus said, "You know that in the world, rulers lord it over their subjects, and their great men make them feel the weight of their authority; but it shall not be so with you. Among you, whoever wants to be great must be your servant, and whoever wants to be first must be the willing slave of all—like the Son of Man; he did not come to be served, but to serve, and to give up his life as a ransom for many" (Matt. 20: 25-28). Those writers who have tried to point this out with any force (John McKenzie is one; have come in for heavy criticism, but what they are saying needs to be stressed: The authority of church leaders is not merely a clerical version of secular authority. It is different, radically different, and the difference is between the world's version of things, which includes power, ambition, rivalry, jealousy, and the assumption that man is a fragmented and unreconciled being; and the Christian way, which proclaims that reconciliation has happened, and God and man are one. Living the consequences of that vision, and shaking off the effects of the world's illusions, are what Christianity is about. Christian leadership should reflect that vision— but that means the same risk the life itself demands, the life Jesus was willing to undertake, and not many people are willing to undertake it. Peter was. It did not make him perfect—we see his

weaknesses plainly, and he prayed and fasted for
the clarity he knew he needed. But his willingness
was total, and because of it he was able to serve
as a genuine leader, whose leadership was not
merely administrative but also, more importantly,
exemplary.

The question associated most with Peter is one
addressed to us. "Jesus asked his disciples, 'who
do men say the Son of Man is?' They answered,
'Some say John the Baptist, others Elijah, others
Jeremiah, or one of the Prophets.' 'And you,' he
asked: 'who do you say I am?' Simon Peter answered: 'You are the Messiah, the Son of the
Living God.' Then Jesus said: 'Simon son of Jonah,
you are favored indeed! You did not learn that
from mortal man; it was revealed to you by my
heavenly Father. And I say this to you: You are
Peter, the Rock; and on this rock I will build my
church, and the powers of death shall never
conquer it.'" (Matt. 16: 13-19).

Although later this passage was used to support
the Roman Catholic idea of the papacy, the Fathers
of the church tended to interpret it in a way which
has relevance for all Christians. The rock which
was the foundation of the church was the confession of Peter that Jesus was the Messiah, the Son
of the Living God. This, Jesus tells Peter, is not
something "learned from mortal man". It must
become part of us, much more than an opinion:
We must work to make it a recognition, so that it is
not something we have heard about and accept at
second hand, but instead it becomes for each of us

something "revealed to you by my heavenly Father." This is the most basic foundation of the church, this recognition which is demanded of all of us.

Peter's failures and recoveries, his rising and falling, finally become the dying and rising of the person who is baptized into the body of Christ. There is always something moving about his nature: his confusion, his loyalty, his cowardice, his bravery, all of the impetuous gestures he makes in the gospel accounts are profoundly human, and in a way he is the easiest apostle to like. But there is something magnificent about the transformed Peter of the Acts of the Apostles, a magnificence which, in a sense, did not end but began with his martyrdom. A story from the apocryphal Acts of Peter became famous again in the novel *Quo Vadis:* Peter, fleeing the persecution in Rome, meets Christ on the road leading into the city. He asks, "Lord, where are you going?" Christ tells him that because Peter is fleeing he is returning to be crucified again. The terrible lesson there—it is one Paul insists upon over and over again—is that all Christians are called on to live the life of Christ, not by imitation but by direct participation, a participation which opens for us with baptism into Christ's body. Peter, a repeated doubter, a sinful and confused man, exhibited that fact in his life and finally in his death. We can applaud this and be moved by it, but we are really in trouble if we stop there. Maybe we are called to try to walk on waters, or to try and fail, and learn the lesson. We are at least called on to try to live with a consistency and undivided attention, the sort of attention which enabled Peter to accept the death in which he was led "where he did not want to go," but by which he also glorified God.

Chapter Five
Paul

One of the most intriguing things about the saints who have left extensive writings is how frequently and intensely they come across as persons. This is certainly true of Paul: He remains a controversial figure. People still find his teachings challenging or repellent enough to get excited over them, even several thousand years after they were first recorded. The man who comes across in the epistles is full of paradox and contradiction—that is to say, he is completely human. Paul shows himself to be authoritarian and humble, loving and angry, boastful and still self-effacing.

He has been blamed for a lot of things, the church among them. For years there has been a charge floating around that Jesus taught one thing, then Paul came along, exploited Jesus' name, and created the institutional church—something Jesus never would have done, according to this line of thought.

Vatican City and the code of canon law may not have been quite what Jesus had in mind, but the fact is that the institutionalization of the church was inevitable, and seemed desirable to the early Christians. I mean by this that they recognized that Christianity was a movement, and it was necessary from the start to make some decisions about the course of that movement. For example, there was at that time a strong gnostic current

throughout the Greek-speaking world, and it made
its influence felt in the early church. Paul was not
the only Christian who encountered it. John was
another apostle who wrote and preached against
it. Another early problem—a more vital one—was
the extent to which the gospel was to be preached.
It was Paul who spread the message to the Gentiles most fervently, and he argued with Peter,
pleading the Gentile cause: Their rights, he said,
were equal to those of the Jewish Christians. None
of these problems was clear-cut. Jesus himself, according to the gospels, sent the disciples out to
preach not to the Gentiles or the samaritans but to
the "lost sheep of the house of Israel". Christianity, with all of its paradoxes, its "love feast,"
its initiation rite of baptism, was suited to the
gnostic notion of special revelation and initiation
into hidden mysteries; and because it was Jewish
by origin and apparently, if the words of Jesus are
taken absolutely literally, by intention, the question of who could belong, and what would be required of those who were believers, was not a
simple one.

The apostles and disciples had to make decisions about issues of this sort, and once decisions are made regarding questions of membership and belief you have an institution. When the
institution is regarded as an end in itself, when it
is not seen as a basically provisional structure
designed to serve larger needs, then it is a burden
and an obstruction, getting in the way of the truth
it was meant to communicate. But this corruption

is part of a process which happens in all sorts of institutions, not only the church, and it is in any case not to be laid at Paul's feet.

However, there is one aspect of the notion that Paul is the author of the church which does have considerable truth. He was not only the best organizer in the early church; he also insisted more strongly than any other apostle that Christianity was a universal message. It was not to be confined to the Jewish community. And although there were Gentile converts to Judaism—we read of several in the gospels and the Acts of the Apostles—they were still considered (and considered themselves) privileged to have been allowed to share in the truth revealed first to the Jews. Paul does not entirely abandon that picture. He reminds the Gentiles in Rome that they are, in effect, privileged to share Israel's natural birthright: "If some of the branches have been lopped off, and you, a wild olive, have been grafted in among them, and have come to share the same root and sap as the olive, do not make yourself superior to the branches. If you do so, remember that it is not you who sustain the root: The root sustains you" (Romans 11: 17-18).

At the same time, it is clear that Paul was aware of the radically universal nature of Christianity. He fought Peter over the issue, and won, when Peter was too cautious and too willing to compromise with those who insisted that Gentile converts to "the new way" observe Jewish ritual. Paul insisted that those who were not born under

the law should not be required to observe it. It was
this direction in the early church which made the
break with Judaism inevitable, because it under-
scored the Christian direction which obliterated a
vital distinction: How could Israel remain pure
and true to its vocation and proclaim, as Paul did,
that "there is no such thing as Jew and Greek,
slave and freeman, male and female; for you are
all one person in Christ Jesus" (Gal. 3:28)? Insofar
as the church is truly universal, Paul's writing and
activity were largely responsible for its being so.

Perhaps the main reason Paul came to be regarded as the corrupter of the church, the one
who allegedly spoiled the pristine message of
Jesus, is the way in which he dominates the Acts
of the Apostles, and because so much in his
epistles *demands*, rather than suggests, a way of
life, a direction which he wanted Christians to
take. At times he even tells his readers that he
knows God's will—a claim which is infuriating
under any circumstances.

The story of Paul's conversion on the road to
Damascus, and the authority he claimed, must
have seemed incredible even to early Christians
who had already accepted the incredible news of
Jesus' resurrection. After all, the other apostles
had been with the movement from the beginning,
had seen Jesus in the flesh. Paul insisted, after the
resurrection and ascension, that he too had had a
vision of the Lord, but his was special—it was an
example of something the church has been suspicious of throughout its history: "special revelation."

A person who claims the sort of authority Paul
claimed, the person who claims a direct knowledge of God's will, as Paul did, is either utterly
mad, or he is a deliberate liar, or he is telling the
truth. Paul in this way is a stumbling block, as
Jesus was.

It is an overwhelming thing, to compare a man
to Jesus; it seems blasphemous to us, just as Jesus'
claims and the claims of his followers seemed
blasphemous to many of the people who first
heard them. But the task which Jesus gave us is
in fact to become what he is, to take on his
nature. "Love one another, as I have loved you,"
he told his followers. "Be perfect, as your heavenly Father is perfect." Throughout the gospels
we are told to forgive as God forgives, to accept
and love one another as we are accepted and
loved by God. It is a radical thing to be told to act
as someone divine acts; it goes to the root of our
lives because we cannot do these things unless we
share, in some way, in the divine life. Over the
years the interpretation of Jesus' counsels has by
and large degenerated into a merely ethical belief:
we are told how a good Christian is to act, and we
act that way, or try to. In the Catholic and Orthodox traditions there is an added sense of participation in the sacramental system: Acts of the
church are understood as mysteries by which
human beings are actually given a share in the
divine life. In a way, however, our conventional
picture of the church involves us in putting the
cart before the horse: The church, in worship
(private as well as communal and sacramental),

grows from a participation which is *already* real;
it is the result of a recognition. The church may be
the cause of that recognition for most of us, but
being a Christian should not be seen primarily as a
matter of behavior (doing what a Christian ought
to do) or sacramental observance. These things
are possible because God calls us to share divine
life every moment, and every moment we can
make a choice to respond, or not to respond. "The
miracle is not that we love God, but that God has
loved us," St. John writes. And because of that
love we are allowed to become, in some way, what
Jesus is: "Here and now, dear friends, we are
God's children; what we shall be has not yet been
disclosed, but we know that when it is disclosed
we shall be like him, because we shall see him as
he is. Everyone who has this hope before him
purifies himself, as Christ is pure" (1 John 3: 2-4).
Christians are called on to be the people who can
look on God's face and live.

The paradox is that as the knowledge of participation in the divine life grows, so does the
knowledge of sin. At its base Christianity is full of
these paradoxes: God becomes man, God goes
through his death as man into hell, the place
where God is not; man begins to become like God
when he admits that he is not God; one-ness with
God begins with the knowledge that we are fallen
—life found when it is lost, God's strength shown
in weakness. Paul exhibits all of these paradoxes
with a kind of furious intensity.

This may be because of the way in which he be-

came a Christian—or rather the way Christ came
to him. For most Christians the life of faith is a
process of deepening, of going within, of growth in
knowledge which happens over the years, as a
result of an openness which is refined and clarified through prayer. For Paul the whole process
was accomplished suddenly—or at least it began
very suddenly—and at the most unlikely time. As
he rode toward Damascus to arrest Christians he
was thrown to the ground by Christ's revelation of
himself.

We know the story and are used to it. It contains
a couple of points which shouldn't be passed over
too quickly, though. One is deeply ironic, and the
irony shows in much of Paul's writing. It is the fact
that the man who was most sincere and whole-
hearted in his opposition to Christianity was
chosen to be its greatest early exponent. It is the
fact that the man, who believed completely in the
righteousness of the law by which man is able to
approach God, was confronted with a God who
took such frightful initiatives—a God whose desire
for Paul was so strong that he could not wait for
Paul to come to him. Perhaps this irony was one
which could be preached most effectively by a
Pharisee. Paul knew that scripture said, "Cursed
be the one who is hanged from the gibbet," as
Jesus was. Something accursed, set apart from
God and man, is salvation for us. God goes where
man did not think even God could go.

The other point is the sort of person God chose
in Paul. As a Pharisee, Paul was passionately de-

voted to the cause of Phariseeism. As long as he
was convinced that Phariseeism was the will of
God he was thoroughly devoted to it, and that
passion is central to his life: As a Christian, he
threw himself completely into the cause of Christianity.

The Revelation of John says, "I know all your
ways; you are neither hot nor cold. How I wish you
were either hot or cold! But because you are
lukewarm, neither hot nor cold, I will spit you out
of my mouth" (Rev. 3: 15-16).

Paul was never lukewarm, not when he stood at
the sidelines approving of Stephen's murder, or
when he rode toward Damascus to see how many
Christians he could bring to justice. Nor is he
lukewarm when he writes, "You stupid Galatians!
You must have been bewitched . . ." (Gal. 3:1), or
when he says of those who demanded circum-
cision for gentile converts, "As for these agitators,
they had better go the whole way and make
eunuchs of themselves" (Gal. 5: 12). A few verses
later he is telling the Galatians, "The harvest of
the Spirit is love, joy, peace, patience, kindness,
goodness, fidelity, gentleness, and self control"
(Gal. 5: 22-23). It is astounding, the way Paul can
turn from wrath to tenderness so quickly. It doesn't
fit at all our usual notion of the saintly man—he
looks more like a brilliant fanatic, which is in fact
the way many critics of Christianity (and a few
Christians as well) have regarded him. That a man
who says that his opponents should castrate themselves can, only a few sentences later, recommend

peace, patience, and kindness is incredible.

Paul is full of these contradictions. He is as full of affection as he is at times full of rage. His letters frequently end with greetings to as many people as he can remember. When he feels that he might have offended his listeners unnecessarily, he is at pains to make himself understood. He can write to the Philippians, "I thank my God whenever I think of you; and when I pray for you all, my prayers are always joyful" (Phil. 1: 3-4). His affection for Timothy is apparent. And it is delightful to see at the end of the letter Paul dictated to the Galatians something spontaneous and tender which has survived every scribal transcription for almost two thousand years: "You see these big letters? I am now writing to you in my own hand" (Gal. 6:11). Paul plainly inspired a similar affection in others. When he said goodbye to the elders of the congregation at Ephesus "there were loud cries of sorrow from them all, as they folded Paul in their arms and kissed him. What distressed them most was his saying that they would never see his face again" (Acts 20: 37-38). Paul even inspired the affection—or at least the respect—of some of those who were allied against him. There is a frustrated friendliness in Festus' outcry during Paul's defense of his actions before King Agrippa: "While Paul was thus making his defense, Festus shouted at the top of his voice, 'Paul you are raving; too much study is driving you mad'" (Acts 26: 24).

Paul's contradictions make him seem larger

than life and a little unpleasant. His character has
been contrasted with that of Jesus; the distinction
usually makes Paul look passionate, boastful,
angry, authoritarian, and places Jesus in the
opposite corner: Jesus is humble, kind, democratic, loving.

This is completely false. "Was Jesus humble? or
did he/Give any proofs of Humility?" asked Wil-
liam Blake, and concluded that as we define
humility Jesus was not humble. Blake also wrote,
"The Vision of Christ that thou dost see/Is my
Vision's greatest enemy . . . Thine is the friend of
All Mankind,/Mine speaks in parables to the
Blind. . . ."

We would like a vision of Christ that contains no
contradiction. Because we are taught by the
church and by tradition that Jesus was God's son
and God is love, we sentimentalize our picture to
remove the moments which contradict this vision
—those moments which might force us to confront
a God whose love is wilder and stranger than the
definitions of love we are comfortable with. Because there are pages and pages of Paul's direct
voice, because his wrath as well as his affections
face us constantly, we have a clearer feeling
about his personality than we are able to have
about Jesus'. There are, however, moments when
we encounter in the gospels a Jesus who looks very
much like Paul. That is the Jesus who, like Paul,
claims something no humble man (no man, I mean,
who is humble in our ordinary gentlemanly definition of the word) would dare to claim unity with

the Father, a unity which led him to claim the
name of God for himself: "Before Abraham was, I
Am." Humility, as we are used to defining it, is not
present in Jesus' response to the news that his
family is waiting for him: "'Who is my mother?
Who are my brothers?' And looking around at
those who are sitting in the circle about him said,
'Here are my mother and my brothers. Whoever
does the will of God is my brother, my sister, my
mother'" (Mark 3: 33-35). We can't avoid the
challenge by saying, "That was all right for him,
he was God." We have to try to see him as his contemporaries must have seen him. What would you
make of a man who called the nation's leader
"That Fox" or denounced respectable religious
leaders as hypocrites, who dared to claim a
special mission from God, and spoke of his unity
with the Father? Our first response to talk of this
sort if it confronted us now would be annoyance or
confusion. We tend to distrust gurus, and we don't
think highly of their credulous followers.

It is also difficult to say that Jesus was always
kind. To say of people who were only trying to fulfill the law of God that they are like tombs painted
white, full of rotting flesh, is not kind. It was not
kind of Jesus to tell a woman who wanted help for
her child that because she was not a Jew he would
not help her, since you do not feed the bread of the
children to dogs. To look exclusively at the Christ
who was a gentle companion to his friends, a man
who was warm with children and forgiving of
sinners, and ignore this arrogant-seeming Jesus,

this authoritarian teacher, is to ignore something
essential in our relationship with God.

We might begin to see what it is by looking at a
line from C. S. Lewis' *Chronicles of Narnia*. Someone asks if Aslan, the lion who is Lewis' Christ-
figure, is a safe lion. And the answer is, "No, he is
not at all safe. But he *is* good."

In another context, Lewis wrote of Christianity
that it had the odd feel of a real thing. If we were
making the planets, he said, we would in all likeli-
hood make them the same size and place them at
equal distances from the sun and from one another.
In fact the universe is wilder and more interesting
than that, and Christianity—with its odd doctrines
of Trinity and Incarnation, its paradoxes—has the
same strangeness about it as the cosmos.

By domesticating Jesus (and in dismissing Paul's
revelation of Jesus we are in danger of doing this)
we are protecting ourselves from a sense of the
strangeness of God, the wildness of his love, which
can appear to us sometimes as anger or arrogance.

This problem of the anger of God—which is reflected in the anger of Jesus and the anger of
Paul—is important to an understanding of the God
who appears in scripture to be capricious and
fickle, as he demands love and fidelity of his
followers. I think that this anger has to be understood as part of what it means to believe in a God
who loves us and wishes to unite himself to us. God
demands the surrender of my whole self; it is only
when I have given myself over to him completely

that he can unite himself with me completely. What does not get united to God is the false self, the idol I have constructed to fool myself and the world with, the thing I build up with my defenses and vanity. That aspect of myself will not leave politely. It is the most tenacious part of what I consider myself. It must be cut through, rather than coaxed away, and anger—an experience of the awe and terror, as well as the love, of God—is perhaps all that can relieve me of the illusion of self-importance.

Sometimes during the course of a friendship or marriage there is a quarrel, a fight, and insult, which at the time of its occurrence seems drastic and unkind. But in the long run it proves helpful. It reveals one or both of the parties in true light, a light which would not have been able to shine if the ordinary rules of civility always prevailed. A quarrel of this sort is never planned. Both husband and wife, or both friends, may be trying their best to be civil under the most difficult circumstances. Finally it becomes impossible, the anger flares up, feelings are wounded, there is remorse on both parts, and in the end the relationship has been clarified. It is stronger and more solid, less illusory, than before. Love is more than civility, and finally it involves the whole range of our perceptions and passions, including anger. If anger can, however awkwardly, be a healing thing at the level of friendship or marriage it will also be a healing thing in our relationship with God.

There are times in a relationship when a quar-

rel of this sort becomes inevitable. But it can't be
done calculatedly—it is especially ugly when one
of the parties tries to improve the other by arrang-
ing things that way. Anger (or anything else) used
manipulatively is profoundly unloving. It reduces
the one who should be beloved to the status of an
object. I don't mean to suggest that the anger of
God is manipulative, the "divine being" stooping
to our level. What I am referring to is the point in a
relationship when someone spontaneously bursts
out, "You have no right to treat me this way,"
revealing the other's insensitivity. The other's
callousness has become an insurmountable barrier, and this becomes apparent to the one who
would love, apparent in a way that wounds, and
spontaneous anger is the result. In Eugene O'Neil's
Moon for the Misbegotten the heroine says to the
drunken, desperate man lying in her arms, "Maybe my love could still save you, if you would only
let it." I am suggesting that God's love for us is this
sort of love. I realize that it is unfashionable to
think of God in these terms, but it is human beings
who are redeemed and joined to God. It must be in
human terms that this process happens. Augustine said of God, "He is nearer to us than we are
to ourselves," and the self which is redeemed is
not merely the rational self, but the self which
dreams, and knows passion, and is angry, and can
be humiliated. The only language we have is the
language spoken by human beings, and any talk
about God will be anthropomorphic, including the
most abstract. Only human beings make abstrac-
tions, after all. And as a friend pointed out to me

once, it doesn't make much sense to worry about anthropomorphic language in a tradition whose central teaching is that God became man.

In confronting Paul's angers and his outbursts of love and ecstasy we confront a man whose passion for Christ was paradoxical and all-inclusive. On the one hand he insists on his own unworthiness, on the other he claims to have been "caught up into paradise" where he "heard words so secret that human lips may not repeat them" (2 Cor. 12: 4). Paul insists, in the same passage, on his own weakness and his authority: "I will not boast on my account, except of my weakness. If I should choose to boast, it would not be the boast of a fool, for I should be speaking the truth. But I refrain, because I should not like anyone to form an estimate of me which goes beyond the evidence of his own eyes and ears. And so, to keep me from being unduly elated by the magnificence of such revelations, I was given a sharp physical pain which came as Satan's messenger to bruise me; this was to save me from being unduly elated. Three times I begged the Lord to rid me of it, but his answer was: 'My grace is all you need; power comes to its full strength in weakness.' I shall therefore prefer to find my joy and pride in the very things that are my weakness; and then the power of Christ will come and rest upon me. Hence I am well content, for Christ's sake, with weakness, contempt, persecution, hardship, and frustration; for when I am weak, then I am strong" (2 Cor. 12: 5-10).

When Paul speaks of God's strength being made

manifest in weakness he indicates something essential to his own theology. Paul is the theologian
of original sin, and we should remember that
original sin, as Christians interpret it, is not an
ancient Hebrew idea. The idea of original sin
dawned with the vision of God's absolutely un-
limited and radical love for man, shown in Christ.
Next to a love so total that it could abandon itself
for the sake of the beloved, man's lack of generosity was revealed starkly.

Much of Paul's authority rests on his use of this
idea: His authority, his strength, is the strength
God demonstrates in Paul's weakness. God chose
an enemy of Christianity to preach Christianity; he
chose a man raised in the love of the law to show
the limitation of the law; he chose a proud man
easily given to anger, and revealed the tenderness, love, and humility which—given a choice—
the unconverted Paul might have kept hidden.

The paradox at the center of the idea of original
sin—that man is at once called on to share God's
life and is at the same time powerless to accomplish that sharing—is an idea which, seen in isolation from the love and generosity of God, can turn
ugly, isolating man in the condition of fallenness.
It makes no sense to isolate this idea, though it is
often done. Fundamentalist Christians frequently
begin with the notion that man is depraved, then
make of God a *deus ex machina*. Beginning with
the fall they overemphasize it, and tell you at the
last moment that there *is* hope after all: uncon-
ditional surrender to the strange God who put you

into this fix in the first place. But I think original sin is more valuably understood as the recognition of our fragmentedness, our cramped and selfish ego-fixation; and this recognition can happen when we recognize God's generosity, when we see that God not only loves man but loves him with an unimaginable passion, a passion which demands a whole-hearted response.

When we begin to have even the dimmest recognition of that love we realize at the same time our own coldness, our lack of response, the insensitivity which governs our lives and responds coolly to God. It cannot be seen apart from the idea of "the prince of this world" spoken of by Jesus. The world in question is not the world of natural things but the world of power, manipulation, and ego. Only an experience of God can throw this world into relief and show it to be the falsehood it is. One experience of this sort threw Paul to the ground on his way to Damascus. It is more gradual for most of us, but just as necessary, and it is the source of true Christian authority. That authority was obvious and powerful in Paul, but it is present to some extent in the lives of all Christians. It is not an authority for which anyone may take credit, and Paul insisted on this point: It was not Paul but the authority of Christ which mattered. St. John the Baptist had said, "He must increase, and I must decrease." Paul said, "Now not I, but Christ lives in me." The life which was witnessed to by both Paul and John is the Christ-life. Jesus was chosen to reveal it, the first of the new men. But

Paul was called on to share it, and to show how unbounded it was. This is the source of his passion—it is as if he had himself gone to the limits of emotion and experience required to know that "there is nothing in death or life, in the realm of spirits or superhuman powers, in the world as it is or the world as it shall be, in the forces of the universe, in heights or in depths—nothing in all creation that can separate us from the love of God in Jesus Christ our Lord" (Romans 8: 38-39).

Chapter Six

Germaine Cousin

Germaine Cousin was born at Pibrac, near Toulouse, around the year 1579. Her father, Laurent, was a poor farm laborer. Her mother died when Germaine was a baby, and her father married again. Neither her father nor her stepmother had any love for Germaine; her stepmother actively despised her. Germaine was sickly, suffered from scrofula, and her right hand was badly deformed. Her stepmother kept her from contact with her healthy brothers and sisters, as if Germaine might contaminate them. She was made to sleep in the stable or under the stairs, was fed on scraps, and she was sent away to mind the sheep in the pastures as soon as she was old enough. She died at the age of twenty-two, after a harsh and desolate life.

What made her a saint? Her life is as bleak an existence as can be imagined.

Saints are scandals—they challenge the way we look at life, at values, at our own Christianity. The enthusiasm and total commitment of Francis of Assisi make our own lukewarm attitudes and our lust for security clear to us.

But there is also something appealing about many of the saints. Thomas More managed to live a quietly ascetic and prayerful life while appearing to be a witty humanist scholar (which of course he was). Teresa of Avila had a sense of

humor which we find completely sympathetic.
Even among the saints who are harder to understand—Ignatius, for example, with his enthusiastic martyrdom, or fierce Agustine—there are
human qualities which we can't help but find
attractive. There is grace in all these lives, not
only in the divine but also in the aesthetic sense of
the word: Their lives are graceful and somehow
attractive. Even their enemies or those who are in-
different to the religious meaning of their lives
would be forced to respect them. Their attractiveness can't be denied by anyone with taste, or at
least an appreciation for dramatic values.

There are millions of human beings who will
never make it into that graceful world because
they can't. They are the people whose lot it is to
make other people uncomfortable, who put people
off with their ugliness, their lack of any attractive
quality, their strange, sudden gestures. We read
about St. Francis kissing the leper, and we are
moved to admiration—for Francis. What about
the leper who allowed himself to be kissed? What
about the person whose unattractiveness is an
absolutely unavoidable cross? We admire the
saint who does not turn his eyes or make sudden
excuses to leave the vicinity of this unsettling
human being—but what about the person himself?
We act as if he had no feelings, as if he were not
aware that people avert their eyes and cross the
street rather than encounter him.

A poet told me once that this tendency to
despise the ugly, to avoid them, to value them less

than others, was the worst thing about the human race. Men and women choose as partners people who appeal to them physically—it is rare that this is not an important consideration; sometimes it is the only one. A person who suffers a disfiguring handicap, or someone who is physically healthy but terribly ugly, can expect mild scorn at least. Even "decent" people will not spend time with such a person if it can be avoided. All of us are guilty of this to some extent. For the most part we don't consider it a moral or spiritual problem: It is only "natural" to react that way.

The puritan conscience of Nathaniel Hawthorne was tormented once by an encounter with a retarded child who held up his arms, wanting Hawthorne to hold him. The child was filthy, ugly, and Hawthorne was revolted. But he did pick the child up, and wrote later that he believed it was a decisive moment in his life: If he had refused that terrible plea, Hawthorne wrote in his journal, he was sure it would have meant his damnation.

We are more sympathetic to Hawthorne's discomfort, when we hear of an incident like this, than we are to the human being who caused it. The photographer Diane Arbus was fascinated by freaks, giants, dwarfs, and other human grotesques. Her pictures are disturbing, frequently unpleasant, always fascinating. When asked why she was intrigued by such people she said, "Most of us spend our lives waiting for the *terrible thing* to happen. For them it has already happened."

Germaine was born on the other side of the terrible thing Diane Arbus talked about. It could be that the solitude she found in the pastures where she tended sheep was the beginning of her holiness. Her piety was conventional enough. She knelt, even in the snow, to say the Angelus; she went to Mass as often as she could, and she often prayed the Rosary. It is remarkable that someone who had been treated so badly would respond to life this way, gratefully and without bitterness, but there is more: She shared what little food she was able to get with beggars.

There are wonderful stories about her. One says that when the river was in full flood, impossible to cross, Germaine wanted to go to Mass. As she walked to the river's edge the waters parted to let her cross, as they had parted for Moses. Another story says that during the middle of a hard winter Germaine's stepmother accused her of hiding stolen bread in her apron and began to beat her; the apron fell open and it was full of fresh summer flowers.

Toward the end of her life, when stories like this were already being told about Germaine, the people of Pibrac realized that there was something extraordinary about Germaine. Her parents began to treat her as a human being, but she chose to live as she always had. According to Butler's *Lives of the Saints*, when her body was accidentally exhumed forty-three years after her death it was perfectly preserved. It was moved into the church sanctuary, and the demand for Germaine's official canonization began.

Look at the contrast between Germaine's life, and the stories. The tales are few, and tell a common story: An ugly person, simple perhaps to the point of simple-mindedness, is despised almost all of her life, which is mercifully short. But it is for such a person that rivers part and fresh flowers bloom in winter. It reminds us very much of a fairy tale, which leads a lot of people to dismiss the sort of story which rose around lives like Germaine's.

Maurice Blondel, the great Catholic modernist, wrote that miracles can be said to prove nothing: to the believer they are wonderful signs which confirm what he already knows through faith, and so he celebrates them. The unbeliever will always be able to find reasons *not* to believe: if the dead were raised before his eyes he would come up with an explanation for it. The understanding of a miracle's significance, Blondel said, happens only where there is a prior faith.

In *Tales From Eternity* (Seabury, 1973) Rosemary Haughton pointed out the resemblance between the world-view of the fairy tale and the world-view of the gospels. To use the similarity as grounds for dismissing fairy tales, or the gospels, or miracle stories, is like having a tin ear for music. People who don't believe in the power of such stories have to deal with the fact that whole religions have been transmitted this way, and some of them were considered dangerous. The gnostic churches which existed from the earliest years of the Christian era until the 13th century went through periods where doctrine was transmitted chiefly through the medium of what we would call fairy tales, and some of these stories survive to this day, although they are no longer seen as threats to the established order.

One interesting thing about fairy tales is the class which produced them. They were told, generally, by people who had very little and lived close to the land. They were the entertainment of the poor, but more; they passed on wisdom, and it was not the wisdom kings care about. A king could hardly expect to be thrilled by the story of a peasant who becomes a king, through magic, virtue, or cleverness. The heroes of fairy tales were usually poor, and the simple minded hero is common. There is, for example, the story of Simple Simon who, because he obeys his mother's instructions with an exasperating and comical literalness, makes a king's daughter laugh, which breaks an enchantment. Of course he marries the princess and becomes a king himself, all the result of his obedience and his foolishness. There is the story of Hans the hedgehog boy. A poor couple give birth to a monstrous child, half human and half hedgehog. They wish for the child's death, but he promises to leave if they will give him a set of bagpipes and a spurred cock to ride on. Through cleverness, treachery, and magic he is finally transformed into a handsome young man who comes into the kingdom which he deserved all along. Those who received him well are rewarded, and those who scorned him because of his ugliness suffer for it.

Fairy tales are not always ethical. Some of the heroes are scoundrels. But they are, like the gospels, tales of transformation, hidden kingdoms, and the ultimate foolishness of wordly wisdom. In them the poor, the meek, the simple, and the merciful often (if not always) inherit the kingdom. Those who are rich and clever in the sight of the world almost always come out badly.

The story of Germaine is like this. It speaks of a kingdom and a power which those around Germaine did not recognize until she made it clear to them. If they had the eyes to see it with, the fact that Germaine was willing to share bread with other hungry people despite the fact that she was often denied bread would have seemed as great a miracle as the parting of the waters. Both works came from the same kingdom, both were animated by the same power. Jesus rejoiced that the kingdom had been revealed to the foolish and hidden from the wise, and Paul writes, "This doctrine of the cross is sheer folly to those on their way to ruin, but to us who are on the way to salvation it is the power of God. Scripture says, 'I will destroy the wisdom of the wise, and bring to nothing the cleverness of the clever.' Where is your wise man now, your man of learning, or your subtle debater —limited, all of them, to this passing age? God had made the wisdom of this world look foolish. As God in his wisdom ordained, the world failed to find him by its wisdom. . . . Divine folly is wiser than the wisdom of man, and divine weakness stronger than man's strength" (1 Cor. 1: 18-25).

All of this is placed by Paul in the context of

Christ's suffering. This suffering reveals the extent of God's love, which in worldly terms is absurd. To be crucified, in the world's eyes, is no way to conquer.

But to be despised, to be ugly or deformed, is worse than being crucified. Anthony Bloom has written that other human beings have suffered more than Jesus, if what you are talking about is human pain. But in his suffering, Jesus went even to hell, the place where God is not, and he rose taking his followers with him. His sufferings do not explain the mystery of evil or suffering, the daily horror which Germaine knew and which others have faced throughout history. But the cross does show that there is a divine involvement in human suffering, that in the abandonment by God which Jesus felt and which millions feel, there is still the work of resurrection.

In demanding fulfillment of people our culture is often very cruel. Almost everyone has encountered someone who suffers because he believes that he is ugly, unattractive to anyone, that his presence makes other people want to get away. Frequently he is told by well-meaning folks that this is not really the case. But in fact there are people who simply are not and never will be attractive, whose manner, for whatever reason, always will make others uncomfortable. The fairy tales and the gospels make more sense here than the school of psychology which holds out worldly hope where there isn't any. (The pitiful and funny passage in Nathaniel West's *Miss Lonelyhearts*, about the girl born without a nose, who wonders what she can do to be like all the other girls, is a good example of the futility and even the cruelty of our usual response to the problems.)

Such people have a right to demand charity, and we have an obligation to give it. It isn't the cold sort of charity I mean, gritting our teeth and doing good deeds, but the charity which comes from understanding that the darkness endured by the grotesque people is our own darkness. Compassion means "suffering with" and charity which stoops from a supposed position of superiority, charity without compassion, is a cold secular politeness which has little to do with the gospel. The gospel, and stories like that of Germaine, reveal a value which is the reverse of the world's, in which the foolish are revealed as wise, and what appears to be weak is strong. As a beginning to this understanding we have to realize that the aversion we feel and consciously or unconsciously direct at the victims of the world comes from the darkness in ourselves and from the wrong, extremely limited standards by which we judge things. It is our own lack of compassion we meet. We are angry that we have been affronted by having to see this sudden unpleasant being, this thing that is so ugly to look at, so discomforting to talk to. One ancient Buddhist writer said that "aversion is a kind of anger, directed at an object." This is true whether the aversion is felt for an insect, the decaying body of an animal, or a hideous human being. It is, in any case, a primitive emotion, but where it is directed at another human being it is a moral offense as well. Even when we try to overcome it, aversion for another human being is usually sensed by the victim, through his consciousness of our averted eyes or our forced smiles. This is what I mean when I say that charity must be a real recognition of his humanity, and not a forced kindness (even though that is plainly better than crossing the street to avoid contact with him).

St. Francis kissed the leper, and we admire him. Francis did not admire Francis, though. We have to look beyond admiration to try to see what he saw. Francis recognized the reality of the kingdom he shared with the leper. Perhaps the leper also understood that Francis embraced him not out of a pity which leans down from above, but embraced him as a true brother. Francis was able to recognize what the world usually cannot: He saw through aversion to the truth. When aversion is understood as part of our own limitation, and not as something that attaches *naturally* to the man or woman in front of us, when we confess to ourselves that it is sin and recognize at the same time that sin has been forgiven, and we can no longer let it bind us, then we might be able to begin to understand that the power which, according to the story of Germaine, parted the waters so that she could cross, is also the power which raised Jesus and reconciles us with all the world's victims, even our own.

Chapter Seven
Ignatius Of Antioch

Apart from the letters which he wrote on his way to death, almost nothing is known about Ignatius. Some historians, following through on a reference in one of his letters, believe he may have been a slave at some point, but Ignatius was probably writing metaphorically there, as he often did. Another tradition says that he was lifted up and carried around by Jesus as a baby—this is because his other name, Theophorus, can mean "God-borne" as well as "God bearer." But this name was more likely one taken by Ignatius at baptism. Still another legend says he was one of the original disciples.

This is all we really know: Ignatius was the third bishop of Antioch, having succeeded Peter's own successor Euodius. He was condemned for his Christianity by Roman magistrates in Antioch, and the sentence was that he should be destroyed by wild beasts in the Roman arena. (The reason Ignatius was sentenced to die in Rome rather than on the spot, in Antioch, was that Rome asked each province to supply a quota of condemned criminals to the Roman circuses, where their execution could be combined with the entertainment of the masses.) Ignatius was led across Asia Minor by ten guards—the number probably means that other prisoners were also being transported with him—and at Smyrna he gave a company of Christians who came to greet him four letters, one for each of the congregations they represented. He wrote three more at Troas before crossing the Mediterranean. Tradition says that he was martyred in the Flavian amphitheatre around 107.

And that is all we know. Ignatius' importance to the church can be found in the letters. They are certainly strange; they are insistent upon the authority of bishops and the necessity of unity between Christians, and weaving throughout this, the earliest defense of episcopal authority, is the strange persistent theme of Ignatius' passionate longing for martyrdom.

It is almost impossible to understand enthusiastic martyrs. Marcus Aurelius thought that suicide was ethically permissible but that it should not be done in a flashy or theatrical manner, and here he referred to the Christians as examples of bad taste in suicide. It *is* very difficult to distinguish between Ignatius' attitude toward martyrdom and suicide. The distinction seems almost legalistic when you read Ignatius' plea to his fellow Christians; he asks them *not* to intercede to save his life, and he is quite insistent about it—so insistent that you are given the impression of a willingness, on the part of the authorities, to spare Ignatius if enough pressure were put in the right places. They were, after all, reasonable men, and in comparison with such men as Marcus Aurelius, Ignatius looks anything but reasonable.

In addition, his insistence on the authority of bishops is odd, coming as early in the history of the church as it does. We frequently think of this emphasis on ecclesiastical structure as a medieval thing, and we wonder how it can have seemed so important to early Christians who, given the murderous opposition of the Roman state, certainly had better things to worry about.

Ignatius defends two perennially and deservedly unpopular causes: enthusiastic martyrdom and excessive clericalism. His letters (and letters attributed to him which later proved to be forgeries) have been used to defend the worst excesses of ecclesiastical self-regard. Any layman who reads Ignatius and doesn't get offended should be ashamed of himself. At times Ignatius seems to be saying that the duty of a layman is to obey clerics without question, and his comparison of the bishop to Christ is hard to swallow, if you have ever met a typical bishop.

Two things have to be borne in mind here. One is that the criterion for the appointment of bishops was not the "old boy network" sort of thing we have had to deal with in recent centuries. (In praising one bishop Ignatius says "his very gentleness is his power," a quality which has not ordinarily been found a qualification for advancement.) The other consideration is that the early Christian church had to deal immediately with threats to its unity. It is important to realize that this unity was not, as it has too often been since, a matter of external conformity. The challenge was to the substance of the church. What did it mean to be a Christian? Who was Jesus—a God who

appeared to be man, in order to tell us something;
or was he truly human? Must followers of the new
way, especially Gentile converts, continue to observe Jewish practices? All of these questions
arose immediately. Ignatius believed that Christianity was the culmination of all religions and the
answer to every human hope, which led to his
rejection of Jewish practice among Christians (he
felt it was looking backward) and he makes the
statement that "Christianity does not look to Judaism, but Judaism looks to Christianity"—a false
statement, historically, but it makes sense within
the terms of his polemic. He goes on to say that
Christianity is a system into which "every other
race and tongue that confesses a belief in God has
now been comprehended."

A more significant challenge was the challenge
of the heresy which became known later as
"docetism"—the belief that Jesus was not really
human, but took on the appearance of humanity;
the incarnation was not real, according to this
view, but apparent, a necessary illusion undertaken for purposes of communication. There was a
deep reluctance to say that God had degraded
himself to our level (for people who believed
docetic ideas the flesh *was* degradation), and consequently some early Christians believed that
human appearance of Jesus was a divinely produced illusion made for our sakes; Jesus was an
instructive phantom who was not born as human
beings are, who did not suffer as we do.

The humanity of Jesus is something Ignatius

insists on: "He was verily and indeed born, and
ate and drank; He was verily persecuted in the
days of Pontius Pilate, and verily and indeed crucified, and gave up his ghost in the sight of all
heaven and earth and the powers of the nether
world. . . . It is asserted by some who deny
God—in other words, who have no faith—that
his sufferings were not genuine. . . . If this is so,
then why am I now a prisoner? Why am I praying
for combat with the lions? For in that case I am
giving away my life for nothing; and all the things I
have ever said about the Lord are untruths"
(Epistle to the Trallians). (This and all quotes from
Ignatius in this chapter are taken from *Early
Christian Writings: The Apostolic Fathers*, Max-
well Staniforth, Ed., Penguin, 1968.)

Orthodoxy, as unfashionable a word as it is,
became important this early in the church: It was
a necessary straining towards purity, a careful-
ness, a deliberate attention to details which might
get blurred in the rush of ideas which swarmed
around the world at this time. The docetic approach to Christ was typical of the hellenism
which found flesh an evil thing; and however
attractive this hatred of flesh might appear to
people who lived in an age when flesh, desire,
disease and death were all more apparently part
of the same dying fabric than they are to our
society, which separates them as easily as that
earlier age included them as part of one decaying
cosmos, however beguiling this vision was, it was
also clear to Ignatius and other Christian teachers

that a denial of the real humanity of Jesus was a denial of what made Christianity unique: the descent of God into flesh, and the elevation of humanity to the level of the divine; the reconciliation of the mortal, dying universe with the eternal, and with the new creation heralded by Christ— all of this was essential, and all of this was eclipsed by docetism, which made Christianity not really a new way, but part of the general swarm of hellenic thought.

During the first several decades of Christianity there were two streams of authority in the church. They were not originally in competition, but the seeds of disagreement were there. One tradition stressed the day-to-day administration and teaching of the church, the other stressed the charismatic and ecstatic aspects of the new way. The apostles themselves were concerned with the first aspect to the extent that they appointed people to oversee and direct the communities they founded, and the overseers (the first bishops) were also the first presiders over the eucharist. The second, more charismatic sort of authority was not as given to organization or the needs of organizers as the first, and from the start it was seen as something that could be abused very easily. But it should be stressed that it was also seen as essential to the functioning of the Christian community. Paul worried about its abuse, but also told his readers, "despise not prophecy." During the first century, the writers of the *Didache* presented a fascinating picture of the organization of the early church, and at the same time they warned Christian communities against charismatic frauds. They also acknowledged charismatic authority—the main point being that it must be put to the test.

But what was the test? Christians were subjected to extraordinary pressures from every side. The state was the most obvious. It could, after all, kill without penalty. There were, in addition, new and eager adherents who were more than happy to drag Christianity into agreement with their own favorite ideological passions.

How, in this situation, were Christians to be sufficiently clear about whatever it was that was essential to Christianity?

It is considered embarrassing theologically, these days, to admit that there are essential things. Granted that these essential things are not denominationally determined (that was the easy way we used to take, confident in *our* right and *their* wrong), it doesn't follow that the whole field of Christianity is open to every reading. The people who believed that Jesus was not human removed him from us; those who defended his humanity were willing to live with paradoxes in order to keep him as the one against whom our human lives are measured.

The fact is that Martin Luther and the Pope would agree about the Nicene Creed. That creed was the result of controversies and victories which were won and lost during the first several hundred years of the church's life. In order to keep the faith clear some authoritative criterion was necessary. The authority of charismatic teachers was too chancy—a heretic could be as exciting as anyone orthodox, and the claim of a teacher to be "speaking in the spirit" was not necessarily a guarantee that the teaching was genuine.

Clement of Rome was the first to make explicit the need for apostolic succession, for an authority which was set aside and consecrated by someone in line with the apostles, the people Jesus himself had sent forth. The occasion of Clement's thought on the subject was an upheaval in the Corinthian church: In the midst of the controversy the old clergy had been deposed and new men took their place. Clement's letter stresses the need for unity and continuity as a source of the order which is the proper context for a church's prayer and thanksgiving.

This need for unity is the source of Ignatius' own teaching, in which the bishop is understood as the representative of God's continued presence in the church. Ignatius' concerns over obedience to the bishop have to be seen in this perspective. The church was a new, terribly exciting, unruly revolutionary movement. The revolution was larger than the political sort—it concerned the whole cosmos, and victory over death. The energy it had liberated was unbounded. At the same time, there was the ever-present and very human temptation to put the energy of this paradoxical, exciting message into the service of your own causes, ideas, and temperamental inclinations.

Jesus could not be an instructive phantom to people who hated the flesh, and a mere man to those who were afraid of the idea that God became human for the sake of human beings. He could not be merciful but not just for the sake of the Marcionites, who hated the God of the Bible but loved Jesus, and just but not merciful for the rigorous Montanists, who were uncomfortable with the idea that Christian forgiveness should know no bounds.

This led to the need for orthodoxy—first, for authoritative people who could serve as ordering, reconciling forces within a community; later for creeds and definitions.

Later, of course, the passion for definition and authority became a new problem. Much of the history of Christianity could be seen as a dialectic between this real need for orthodoxy and order, and the recognition that order and obedience are not the essence of Christianity. Ignatius believed that the bishop was essential to the church, and given the situation he had to deal with, he was right. But a couple of centuries later a lay movement which we know now as monasticism began, and one of its first great thinkers, Cassian, could write that it was a saying of the monastic fathers that a monk should avoid women and bishops, since neither would give him any peace.

In its context, Ignatius' defense of the episcopacy is understandable. His passion for martyrdom is not. I don't think it will ever be an attractive idea. Thomas More did everything legal to

avoid it, accepting it only when there was no
alternative but the lie he could not say. In Ignatius' case we have this: "I am yearning for
death with all the passion of a lover." This line
occurs in his Epistle to the Romans, a poetic
defense of his need for martyrdom (it is, strangely,
the one epistle in which he does not make a strong
plea for the episcopacy), and it is in this letter that
he wrote the line for which he is most famous: "I
am His wheat, ground fine by the lions' teeth to be
made the purest bread for Christ."

Can we ever consider this healthy, however
stirring and powerful it may be? Not if we think of
it in terms of ordinary expectations. If we see our
lives as limited by old age, disease, or fatal
accident, with the time between filled with every
possibility; if we think that our purpose in living is
to take advantage of those possibilities, making
the most of what we are offered; then the desire
for death (especially one as unpleasant as being
mauled and eaten by lions) is certainly unhealthy.

If, on the other hand, we see death as an inevi-
tability, one which will in any case be unpleasant;
and if we are at the same time expecting the
coming of Christ, who will want a clear sign of our
allegiance; and if we believe that the same power
which raised him from the dead is at work among
us; then this sort of death will make more sense.
The early Christians prayed for the coming of
Christ, and they meant it in historical terms. They
believed that he was coming soon; his coming
would mean the transformation of everything.

They believed that having been baptized into Christ's death they were also participants in his resurrection, part of the new order of things. That new order was made manifest to the world only through the death of Christ and the deaths of his followers, who, like Christ, were destined for glory in the new creation of which Jesus was the herald.

Christians saw themselves as a people whose lives were a vital part of God's transforming work, a work which involved all life and all death. They fought for the transformation of everything. "For the work we have to do is no work of persuasive speaking," Ignatius wrote. "Christianity lies in achieving greatness in the face of the world's hatred."

The world's hatred against which Christians had to achieve greatness was part of the demonic opposition to the power of the resurrection. That hatred was undeniable: Christians saw it graphically demonstrated every day. If Ignatius seems paranoid, consider the fact that they really *were* out to get him, and his brothers and sisters of the New Way. This persecution confirmed their apocalyptic view of the world, strengthening their desire to make their message and its power clear to the world. Since the prophets and Jesus were persecuted and killed, his followers owed it to the divine tradition they were part of to die worthy of the heritage they dared to claim. It was a cosmic war they were engaged in. To ask, in the face of this worldview, whether Ignatius' desire for martyrdom was "healthy" is beside the point. It was, given the intensity of his condition, almost inevitable. If you are an honest man involved in warfare with every evil power which ever lived, your first concern is not saving your skin. "No power, visible or invisible, must grudge me my coming to Jesus Christ. . . . He who died for us is all I seek; He who rose again for us is my whole desire. The pangs of birth are upon me; have patience with me, my brothers, and do not shut me out from life, do not wish me to be stillborn. Here is one who only longs to be God's; do not make a present of him to the world again. . . . Suffer me to attain to light, light pure and undefiled; for only when I am come thither shall I be truly a man."

Here Ignatius sounds like Paul, who speaks in the epistle to the Romans of all nature groaning with the pangs of birth, waiting for the universe to be born; and it is like the passage in Revelations, in which God gives to each of the faithful a stone upon which is written his true name. In Eastern Orthodox theology grace is understood in these terms: It is a cooperation with the process of birth, a kind of midwifing done by human beings and God together, and it brings about the kingdom of God. Ignatius celebrates this in his Epistle to the Ephesians: "Mary's virginity was hidden from the prince of this world; so was her child-bearing, and so was the death of the Lord. All these three trumpet-tongued secrets were brought to pass in the deep silence of God. How then were they made known to the world? Up in the heavens a star gleamed out, more brilliant than all the rest. . . . Great was the ensuing perplexity; where could this newcomer have come from, so unlike its fellows? Everywhere magic crumbled before it; the spells of sorcery were all broken, and superstition received its death-blow. The age-old empire of evil was overthrown, for God was now appearing in human form to bring in a new order, even life without end. Now that which had been perfected in the Divine counsels began its work; and all creation was thrown into a ferment over this plan for the utter destruction of death."

Ignatius' death was to be one more utterance of God, another participation (like that of the Prophets) in the eternal Word which was made manifest in Christ and which worked for universal transformation. Martyrdom may not seem to us to be a healthy response to this news, but we have to understand the excitement and the total commitment of communities who believed that they were directly assisting in this transforming work. "I shall never have a better chance than this of getting to God," Ignatius wrote to the Romans in an effort to keep them from trying to save his life. "By staying silent and letting me alone, you can turn me into an intelligible utterance of God; but if your affections are only concerned with my poor human life, then I become a meaningless cry once more."

However strange his attitude towards his martyrdom was, what Ignatius says here is true. Martyrs as different as Ignatius and Thomas More are "utterances of God," expressions of divine life among us. Justin Martyr, in arguing for Christianity against the paganism of the Empire, pointed out that never before had very common people gone to death for their beliefs with such joy, as if there were an amazing power at work among them . . . the power that had raised their teacher from the dead into a transformed human life. That transformation was what Justin sought, and his death was a sign (to Justin as well as to those who saw him die) that his belief in the promise of resurrection was wholehearted. It was not a death-wish which motivated him, but a life-wish of a peculiar sort, peculiar because we find his insistence on martyrdom paradoxical, a too-literal interpretation of "He who seeks his life will lose it, and he who loses his life will find it." Still, the problem with interpretations which are not literal enough is that they can water down the force of the message. And in any case we are called on to know what Ignatius knows: that we must be singleminded about attaining to "light pure and undefiled; for only when I have come there shall I be truly human."

Chapter Eight

Justin

In its early years Christianity must have looked frantic and unreasonable to many puzzled Romans and Greeks of good will. Starting out as an apocalyptic Jewish heresy the new religion spread like wildfire. What it offered was a proclamation, rather than a reasoned argument, and the proclamation was an either/or sort of thing which appealed to slaves and women, and amazingly enough to a few intelligent people. But the message left a lot of people in the dark. It was known that Christian rituals were held secretly and non-believers were not admitted to them. And there were terrible rumors about the Christians: They held orgies, defended incest, practiced human sacrifice and cannibalism—these were a few of them. They were also apparently seditious, preaching the equality of slaves, disputing absolute property claims over wives and children and slaves. As reasonable a man as the good stoic emperor Marcus Aurelius despised and persecuted them.

Christians were reluctant to reveal their sacred mysteries to a public which believed such distortions and outright lies about them. Because the Mass was considered too sacred a thing to be done in the presence of non-believers, a certain credence was lent to the rumors: Why would they insist on secrecy if they weren't hiding something?

There is a remnant of the early Christian attitude in a prayer said before communion during the Orthodox liturgy: "I will not speak of your mysteries to the enemy, nor betray you, as Judas did, with a kiss, but rather pray as the thief did: Lord, remember me when you come into your kingdom."

Then a new sort of teacher arose: the apologist, whose teaching was not addressed primarily to believers but rather to a world which not only did not believe, but accepted the most incredible lies about Christianity.

Justin is the earliest apologist whose writings have come down to us. He was born around the year 100, and was martyred about 65 years later in Rome. Although he was born in Palestine his family was Greek; they were well-to-do pagans who gave their son an excellent education. Justin was at first enthralled with rhetoric, poetry, and the study of history, but after awhile he turned with passionate enthusiasm to the study of philosophy. His first inclination was to stoicism, but as good as the stoics were where ethical teaching was concerned, they could tell him nothing about God, so he looked to other philosophies. Neither the Pythagorean nor the Aristotelian system held him long—he was especially put off by one teacher's eagerness for payment—and he finally thought that he had found what he needed in Platonism. Its teachings about the Logos and the ascent of the soul to God answered his thirst for truth.

One day as Justin walked through a field he met

an old man and struck up a conversation. Justin began speaking of Plato's thought, and the old man told him that an even more exalted philosophy was the one revealed by God to the prophets, the revelation which reached its culmination in Christ. He encouraged Justin to pray for the knowledge revealed by God rather than men. Justin had always suspected that the rumors about Christians were gross distortions or lies, and now he was more eager than ever to study their scriptures and teachings. At about the age of thirty he was baptized, and began his career as an apologist for Christianity.

Justin was convinced that human beings were, above all, rational, and that if Christianity were presented correctly many would return to it. At the very least the persecution of Christians would cease. Wearing the cloak of a philosopher, Justin traveled from city to city and country to country, setting forth not only the teachings of Christianity but, in a radical departure from earlier Christian practice, describing in his apologies exactly what happened at the meetings of Christians. He debated with philosophers of all persuasions and with adherents of every religion he encountered in his travels. In Rome, Justin debated the Cynic philosopher Crescentius, and Eusebius writes that it was because of Crescentius' envy that Justin was arrested during his second visit to Rome; this may not be the case, since the trial accounts contain no hint of any special persecution directed at Justin. Being Christian was crime enough.

Justin was beheaded along with five other men
and women, having refused to sacrifice to the gods
as a sign of submission to the total authority of
Rome. His response to the authorities, when they
asked him to save his life by offering the sacrifice,
was worthy of the philosopher he had always
claimed to be: "No right-minded man forsakes
truth for falsehood."

Two of Justin's apologies are in existence; they
are reasonable works, far from the exuberant,
triumphant Christian writing we see in the works
of Ignatius of Antioch. But the difference was in
the audience: Ignatius wrote to his Christian
companions; Justin addressed the Emperor and
other highly placed Roman authorities. The tone of
his letters is one of confidence in their fair-
mindedness. It is also an uncompromisingly bold
demand for an honest hearing.

Justin presents his plea to the Emperor An-
toninus Pius "in behalf of those men of every race
who are unjustly hated and mistreated," and he
considers himself one of them. He points out that
truly good men, lovers of wisdom, must honor only
the truth and abandon even the most revered
customs of their forefathers, if they are worthless.
We are obliged not only to avoid falsehood; "the
lover of truth must choose, in every way possible,
to do and say what is right, even when threatened
with death." (This and other quotes from Justin
are taken from *Readings in Church History*, edited
by Colman J. Barry, O. S. B., Newman, 1960.)

Pointing to the injustices Christians had been

forced to endure, the unfairness of the processes used against them in the courts, and the refusal to investigate the truth of the charges against Christians, Justin proceeds to offer in refutation of those charges a clear picture of the Christian life. The similarities to our own churches are fascinating; some of the differences should shame us.

In explaining Christian practices, Justin begins with Baptism and the Eucharist. Those who have come to believe in the teachings of Jesus and believe that they can follow the life demanded by Christianity "are taught in prayer and fasting to ask God to forgive their past sins, while we pray and fast with them." Then they are baptized, and the eucharist is celebrated; it consists of common prayers for the church and for all humanity, at the conclusion of which the believers kiss. Then bread and watered wine are offered with lengthy prayers of thanksgiving. All share the bread and wine, and deacons take it to the ones who are absent. "Not as ordinary bread or as ordinary drink do we partake of them," Justin writes. Comparing the transformation of bread and wine to the incarnation of God in flesh, he says that the eucharistic bread and wine are "both the flesh and blood of that Jesus who was made flesh."

So far there is some resemblance between the contemporary church and the church of the first followers of Jesus, though we have lost the sense of brotherhood which led them to pray and fast with those who are looking for truth. Where are the differences?

"Henceforward," Justin writes, "we constantly remind one another of these things. The rich among us come to the aid of the poor, and we always stay together." Justin describes the collection which is taken for strangers, the poor, captives, the sick, "in short, for all those in need." This was seen as an essential part of being Christian during the first years, and it was pointed out even by their opponents as an amazing thing. But it diminished as Christianity grew respectable. During the patristic era it had declined to such an extent that Ambrose and John Chrysostom preached fiery sermons, trying to get Christians to understand that work for the poor and suffering is at the center of Christian living.

It is easy to understand how respectability corrupts. No one feels comfortable helping prisoners or the poor, unless the help is channeled through a non-offensive sort of charity, something like the United Fund or Community Chest. It must look like something any good citizen would do, and as far as it goes this help isn't indecent. But it is also the sort of charity which leaves everything as it is: The prisoners remain in prison, the poor remain poor, help is seen as material benefit only, done for "those less fortunate" by "those more fortunate." Nothing is seriously questioned. The old order doesn't pass away; it gets a moral face-lift. I don't mean to suggest that the first Christians were simply social revolutionaries, but their lives and their works were signs of a new order, a radically different way of viewing the world. To them the world of the poor was not the world of those "less fortunate" but a place where the poor were blessed brothers and sisters. They acted on that insight.

It may be that this world is invisible to us until our own becomes, for whatever reason, intolerably oppressive. Perhaps this is why our churches and churchgoers look bland and purposeless next to the Christians who insist on their belief while living under threat of death. For trying to speak honestly in Russia, Alexander Solzhenitsyn is exiled. His fierce orthodoxy is too great a threat to the government to allow him a place there. President Park of South Korea sees a threat in the work done for the poor by Bishop Daniel Chi and his friend the Catholic poet Kim Chi Ha. While church people in our country wonder what their role is, circumstances have forced clarity on these others. The danger to Christianity here is more subtle. Our society tolerates the church; the government has even made it a mascot of sorts. But when Christians actively try to challenge the state's right over life and death, as some did during the war in Vietnam, they are called subversive. In a sense they are. There is as great a threat to any government in this challenge to its absolute authority as there was to Roman Imperial authority; the judges who have faced Christians throughout the ages will sympathize with the magistrate who had to deal with the Christian slave Euelpistus, a man martyred with Justin, who told the magistrate "I am freed by Christ." There is a challenge to all authority involved in any human being's claim that something matters more than the rule of the people and institutions "in charge". The challenge makes Christianity look like an ally of social revolution—until the revolutionaries win, at which time it becomes plain that Christianity is a perpetual ideological misfit. This spirit, though, is what keeps the world honest, wherever it *is* honest; here the metaphor occasionally used about Christianity—that it acts as a leaven in the world, a hidden necessary thing—takes on a renewed meaning. During the Nazi era in Germany the Jews presented a challenge to the state's absolute rule simply by being there, a people who could not be used as easily as every institution in the country was used. Will Herberg has underlined the fact that the Jews were an obstacle to Nazism simply because they were Jews; the Christians who presented an obstacle were the handful who were faithful.

Apart from the few there was a massive acquiescence to Nazism in which the churches played a leading role. The eagerness of the churches to go along with Hitler was fed by the state's willingness to allow them to exist—so long as they existed in a vacuum. *Noblesse oblige* on both sides; the church makes a lovely pet once it has been fixed.

This is the problem with the churches in America and other democratic countries. So long as church praises state and state praises church they get along well. Church property is tax-exempt, church leaders open sessions of congress with a prayer, and during sermons they speak of "restoring our nation's moral fiber" and "returning to the values on which this country was founded." This idolatrous identification of the state with the purposes of God has become such a convincing mutual admiration society that many will ask what is wrong with it.

The problem in Justin's time was different. Establishment religion in those days was not Christianity but decadent paganism. Sacrifice to the gods and being a good citizen went hand in hand. The people who did not sacrifice to the accepted gods were threats. At times Christians tried to prove that they were moral, as if morality and good citizenship were the same thing. Here the state was more sophisticated. It understood that the issue was not really public order or morality, but allegiance. "Jesus is Lord," Christians said, where the state said "Caesar is Lord."

The problem comes down to allegiance—serving both God and Mammon being desirable, from Mammon's point of view but not from God's—and it occurs again and again throughout the history of the church. In the case of many Christians (Thomas More, Ignatius, Justin, Solzhenitsyn, Fr. Delp, Helder Camara, Dorothy Day) it has taken the form of confrontation with the state; but other institutions play the same role; John of the Cross was imprisoned by members of his own religious order, and Francis of Assisi felt compelled to leave his own family. Any institution can demand an allegiance the Christian must refuse, and the refusal might be dangerous, or heartbreaking. Our celebration of the lives which such committed men and women have lived should lead us to question our own allegiances and commitments. When asked by the prefect what doctrines he held, Justin answered, "I have endeavored to make myself acquainted with all doctrines, but I have given my assent to the true doctrines of the Christians, whether they please the holders of false beliefs or no." His courageous rejection of falsehood here is united with the openness that characterized his life. He was able to search for and embrace the truth with incredible confidence, but this truth is something he arrived at because of an openness which led him to look seriously and sympathetically at a number of alternative philosophical and religious systems. Today there is a fundamentalism which sees in every non-Christian religious system the direct work of Satan.

Although Justin at times seems to echo this view (he claims, for example, that demons inspired the Mass-like ritual performed by Mithraic believers, who offered bread and water which had been consecrated) his openness towards other thought-systems is a far cry from fundamentalism. Justin undeniably believed that Christianity was true in an absolute, blindingly radiant way. All other thought systems, he believed, were revealed as inferior to Christianity when a reasonable comparison was made; but sometimes that falsehood was no more than the omission of Christ, and it is plain that this was seen less as the work of demons than the mysterious work of historical distances. Justin looked not only at divergences from Christian truth—he was far more interested in similarities, which he believed were signs of the working of God in every search for truth. Justin believed that the Word of God was to some degree accessible to anyone who looked for truth. Here he made use of the platonic idea of the Logos, the mediating power between God and the world.

By living in the light of truth (wherever it appeared, from Christian, Jewish, or Greek sources), truth-seekers incurred hatred. This fact was the cornerstone of Justin's defense of Christians. "We know that the followers of the Stoic teaching, because they were praiseworthy in their ethics, as were also the poets in some respects, because of the seed of reason implanted in all mankind, were hated and killed. As examples, we could mention Heraclitus . . . and Musonius, of our own times, and others. For, as we pointed out, the demons always brought it about that everyone who strives in any way to live according to right reason and to avoid evil be an object of hatred. . . . Christ, who appeared on earth for our sakes, became the whole Logos, namely, Logos and body and soul. Everything that the philosophers and legislators discovered and expressed well, they accomplished through their discovery and contemplation of some part of the Logos."

Justin considered Socrates "the most ardent" of those who sought the Logos. He urged his accusers

to consider the fact that Christians were accused
of the same crimes Socrates was accused of. But
here was a difference: "There was no one who
believed so much in Socrates as to die for his
teaching, but not only philosophers and scholars
believed in Christ, of whom even Socrates had a
vague knowledge (for He was and is the Logos who
is in every person, and who predicted things to
come first through the prophets, and then in
person when assumed our human nature and
feelings, and taught us these doctrines), but also
workmen and men wholly uneducated, who all
scorned glory, and fear, and death. Indeed, this is
brought about by the power of the ineffable Father,
and not through the instrumentality of human
reason."

This is far from fundamentalism. Justin even
speaks of the "participation in the seminal Divine
Word" of people like the Stoics and Socrates.
What relevance does this have to our age? Plenty:
Whenever there are people who insist that an
appreciation of Buddhism or Hinduism or Judaism
is a work of darkness, Justin serves as a counter-
weight. There are people who think this way, who
insist that theirs is the *real* old-time religion; yet
here is Justin, writing before the New Testament
was a determined thing (he calls the readings from
Christian writers the "memoirs of the apostles")
preaching a Logos which was never so easily
confined. Justin sounds as modern as Thomas
Merton when he writes, "I am proud to say that I
strove with all my might to be known as a Chris-

tian, not because the teachings of Plato are different from those of Christ, but because they are not in every way similar. . . . The truths which men in all lands have rightly spoken belong to us as Christians."

Justin's openness led him not only to Christianity, if Christianity is seen in sectarian terms, but to an appreciation of the Word of God which transcends the boundaries of any religion. For him the Logos of John the evangelist and the Logos of Plato were not separate, but different only in that one writer had his appreciation of the universal Logos enriched by his encounter with that word made flesh. The fact that this truth he sought all his life, the Logos he knew first in his desire for truth and found expressed in Plato's system, had become flesh—that fact gave Justin courage. He was a catholic in the root sense of the word, a universalist who saw in Jesus Christ the inexpressible truth of God made manifest in flesh. The wisdom he found there gave him the courage to die, as it gave Socrates courage. Justin believed that what Socrates knew and died for had been vindicated by Jesus. "For," he wrote, "we worship and love, after God the Father, the Word who is from the Unbegotten and Ineffable God, since he even became man for us, so that by sharing in our sufferings He might also heal us."

Chapter Nine
Benedict

Gregory the Great, Benedict's biographer, calls him "the man of God." Though we think of him primarily as a monk and the father of monasticism in the west, Gregory's phrase is a better description of him than any. It simplifies things by cutting through our image-laden notion of monastic life (the robes, the silence, long shadowy cloisters) to the basic reasons for monastic living. Those reasons are stated early in the rule Benedict wrote: "In the first place whatever good work you begin, ask him with earnest prayer to perfect it . . . because we must always serve him with the good things he has given us. . . . Let us rise, finally, since scripture tells us: 'It is time now to rise from sleep.' Now that our eyes are open to the deifying light, let us hear what the divine voice tells us daily."

Gregory's life of Benedict is full of accounts of his miraculous works, and while the miracle stories tell us something about the man, the knowledge we have of him is surprisingly sparse, given the tremendous influence he has had. We know that he was born in Norcia, in Umbria, around the year 480, and that he was sent as a young man to Rome, to complete his studies. Rome's decadence made him conclude that a Christian life could not be lived there without unnecessary difficulty, and at about the age of twenty he became a monk.

living alone at Subiaco. His reputation grew
rapidly; a community of monks heard of him and
asked him to be their abbot. We are told that they
changed their minds about Benedict's authority so
radically as to want to see him dead—they tried to
poison him. Benedict returned to Subiaco, and
over the years he organized twelve communities
of monks, finally settling at Monte Cassino, a
community he directed personally. It was for this
community that he wrote the rule for which he is
best known, and he died there, around 547.

These are the main facts. What makes them
important to us now? What relevance can a saint
of the fifth and sixth centuries have to our age—
especially one whose life was dedicated to monasticism, a calling which seems to many Catholics a
waste of good men?

I know it is unfashionable, but I believe that an
understanding of monasticism is one of the most
important works facing the church. I don't mean
by this a defense of monasticism in its traditional
forms, but rather an understanding of the impulse
which drove the first monks away from the cities
into deserts. I believe that monasticism is not a
cop-out, an abandonment of a suffering world for
the sake of personal perfection, but that it is
instead a radical attempt to undertake the life
suggested by the beatitudes.

During the third century Christian monasticism
became apparent. I put it that way because to say
it "began" then implies that it was a foreign thing,
something extraneous to a purer form of Chris-

tianity in earlier ages; and this would be mis-
leading. The common life, asceticism, and the
pursuit of singleminded devotion are all to be
found in the New Testament. But by the third
century the circumstances of Christianity had
changed in a way which made monasticism a
necessary thing. As a specific, separate vocation
it *was* new to Christianity, and it is easy to see
why it was as shocking to some Christians of that
age as it remains today: Jesus had told his followers
to preach the word of God everywhere, and now
some of them seemed to be running in the opposite
direction. It has been asked in almost every age
whether a man living alone in the desert can be
said to be following Jesus' call. Isn't it an unchris-
tian fastidiousness to be so shocked at the corruption of society that you flee it, as Benedict is
alleged to have done? Wouldn't the Christian task
be one of evangelization, not retreat?

C. S. Lewis wrote somewhere that there is a
tendency in an age obsessed with one vice to warn
against the opposite vice; so in an age excessively
concerned with sex, people are warned against
puritanism, and in a puritanical age people are
warned about lasciviousness, each age avoiding its
own problem in this fashion. In judging a phenomenon like monasticism we have to keep this in
mind. Is it really in Christian terms that the
decision to leave a society for the monastic life
shocks us? Or does the shock occur at a less noble
level? Are we bothered because the monk leaves
the poor and suffering people of the world, or

because he leaves us, and the life we have chosen for ourselves? This should lead to another question. Our criticism of the monk implies that by staying in the world we have made the better choice. What are we doing for the suffering world we accuse the monk of leaving? Or is this another case of serious Christianity being for others to undertake?

The decision of the monk raises questions for us, but it also raises questions for the monk. A central question is of course the one already referred to: Is this an abandonment of the Christian task? As uncomfortable as the desert is, it beats hell out of Harlem. It is very difficult being alone for long periods of time, but it is much more difficult to clean the sores of grotesques who are made in God's image and who die far away from the desert.

I doubt that many monks make it through more than a few months of monastic life without being faced with these questions and many more. But an even more basic question is, what is it that is left, and what is sought? When people speak of monks "leaving the world," what do they mean? Obviously monks remain on the planet, so it is not the world God created that they leave—and this is part of the point.

When monasticism began to show itself in Christianity the religion preached by the Christian church had already become fairly well established. It was composed of a number of disparate currents, it was about to be legalized, and there were now Christians in the upper echelons of society. It would be increasingly difficult, as the years passed, to separate being an orthodox Christian from being a supporter of whatever ruled the society at large—whatever emperor, set of values, or political considerations—and in this way the identification of the church with power and the values of society became a new danger. Christians at least had to tolerate these evils if they were to live easily within any society. The anonymous *Epistle to Diognetus* had said of Christians that they lived in every country as if they were aliens, but this was becoming less and less the case. The identification of the church with the powers which surrounded it became a new danger, one which did not die with the Roman empire. It has continued into our own day, where Billy Graham's courtship of presidents and Cardinal Spellman's uncritical enthusiasm for U.S. military policy have been among its recent incarnations.

But there are other less obvious (and maybe more dangerous) ways in which the church and the world live together. There is something heavy and obvious about political or ecclesiastical corruption, and since few of us are involved directly in either it makes an easy target. There is a more immediate danger for most of us: That is the reduction of Christianity to an attitude surrounded by rules and controls, the attempt to make something comfortable and more or less predictable of a message which is in fact unbounded and rather wild. When preachers speak of Christian morality they usually have sexual morality in mind, for example, or crime in the streets; but Christian morality also says, sell all you have, die to yourself, love your enemies, be perfect as your heavenly Father is perfect. We keep the most obvious negative recommendations of Christianity in mind (Thou shalt not kill) and qualify them when the surrounding society asks us to (Thou shalt not kill except in the cases of war and capital punishment); and we underplay or ignore the radical demands found in the beatitudes and the rest of the sermon on the mount.

The problem with the beatitudes, though, is that they do not involve a determined effort on our part so much as they involve being open to the will of God, and attentive to the work of the Holy Spirit.

There are a couple of things which fight that attention. One is the fact that comfort and power are self-centering things. They make us pay nearly constant attention to our own desires and the ability we have to make events happen the way we want them to. The other thing is related: Very often the things we have to do to "make a living" (that phrase is revealing) distract us constantly, and make attention impossible.

When Antony, the father of Christian monasticism, left his comfortable home in Egypt during the later part of the third century it was this world he was leaving—the world of self-regard, power, and distraction. He was not fleeing from Christian obligation so much as he was trying to return to it, radically, by breaking with everything which stood in the way. To do this he left the city for the desert.

Our current picture of monastic life is one of a quiet, organized, peaceful, clerical world, a world of whitewashed walls and orderly activity. But at the root of the monastic experience lies something different. In the first place, monasticism was at the root a lay movement. Antony was not a priest, nor was Benedict nor were most of the early monks. In the second place, the "peace which passes understanding," the peace sought by the monks, is not a peace which comes easily, in cloisters or anywhere else. Many early writers speak of the monks leaving the world to go into "wild places". As they realized, when you go into a wild place what you find is danger. Some of those dangers were physical—wild animals and outlaws—but there were more basic, personal dangers. According to the legend of St. Antony, he was confronted with every imaginable temptation, and overcame them. There are dramatic paintings of this; I think they are too dramatic, because they make it seem that temptation is something extraordinary and not the most ordinary thing in the world. It is in turning around to confront the danger that the monk differs from other people.

It is too bad that the emphasis traditionally put on sexual conduct has reduced our use of the word "temptation". Many of us think of sexual temptation when we hear it; maybe we think,

occasionally, of being tempted to anger. This only
goes to show our insensitivity to any but the most
obvious temptations, the ones which cause physical sensation. What about the self-importance
which is such a constant accompaniment that we
notice it only when someone takes us less seriously than we take ourselves—at which point our
outrage fills the world? Until we force ourselves,
or until we are forced by circumstances, to be
still in a quiet place, we are unaware of how
completely we are led around by self-will and our
own desire; we are unaware of how much of
what we ordinarily think of as "me" is made up
of noise. Our minds are so scattered and in-
attentive that the possibility of hearing God's will
or understanding a neighbor's real need is very
slight.

It is a responsive clarity and singlemindedness
which is the goal of monasticism. This is the
answer to the question of whether the monk has
abandoned the Christian calling. He is trying first
to be Christian; what a Christian does will follow
that, naturally. Before doing what Christians are
to do, you have to leave all you have—and that
means a lot more than material possessions.

As good as this is, still it raises the question:
Isn't this a selfish form of soul-polishing? How is
the world helped by monks?

Setting aside the fact that there were times
when monasteries were directly involved in
feeding the poor, the question can be answered
in several ways. The monastery is a judgement on

the world. The Russian abbot Theodosius not only made sure that his monks kept to the contemplative life, and also that they fed the poor and cared for the sick; in addition he frequently rebuked the wealthy and the powerful for their indifference to the needs of the poor. His monastery was always open to the poor, and closed to everyone else. "Even the prince of Kiev had to ask for special permission to enter," writes Helene Iswolsky (*Christ in Russia*, Bruce, 1960), "and he did not always obtain it." The monks were not allowed to accumulate anything beyond what was strictly necessary for life; anything more had to be given to the poor.

This attitude stems from something even more basic to Christianity: singlemindedness. The tendency among Christians in every age has been to make a partial thing of Christianity. A person has several "lives": a business life, a love life, a religious life. This was not at all the attitude of the early church, but as Christians found it easier to live in the larger society this compartmentalization increasingly became a feature of Christian consciousness, and it remains with us. Even while we may not admit this in theory, it is true in practice. Most of our day is not spent in a state of mind which allows prayer to happen; when we do try to pray it is with a certain self-conscious deliberation; we come to it "from outside." This is far from Kierkegaard's definition of purity of heart—"to think one thing"— and it is in order to think one thing, to *be* one

thing, that a person becomes a monk. That fact
alone is helpful to the larger church. In the first
place, it tells us that it is possible. In the second
place, people who do make this radical break
with everything that stands between themselves
and God can tell us things that are helpful, things
which we need to know about prayer. In the
Russian church, men who have spent their lives
in solitary prayer open their cells toward the end
of their lives to anyone who needs help or advice,
and in the west, monasteries have been important centers of spirituality for the whole church.

In his *Raids on the Unspeakable* (New Direc-
tions, 1964) Thomas Merton, writing of the sixth
century Syrian monk Philoxenos, says, "there is
no explanation and no justification for the solitary life, since it is without a law. To be a
contemplative is therefore to be an outlaw. As
was Christ. As was Paul. One who is not 'alone,'
say Philoxenos, has not discovered his identity. . . .
Now if we take our vulnerable shell to be our true
identity, if we think our mask is our true face, we
will protect it with fabrications even at the cost
of violating our own truth. This seems to be the
collective endeavor of society. . . . In order to
experience yourself as real, you have to supress
the awareness of your contingency, your unre-
ality, your state of radical need. This you do by
creating an awareness of yourself as *one who
has no needs that he cannot immediately fulfill.*
Basically, this is an illusion of omnipotence: an
illusion which the collectivity arrogates to itself,

and consents to share with its individual members in proportion as they submit to its more central and more rigid fabrications."

This is the society which the monk leaves; the world he leaves behind is the world of illusion. However it is accomplished, the liberation sought by the monk is necessary for all. And this emancipation, Merton writes in the same essay, "can take two forms: first that of the active life, which liberates itself from enslavement to necessity by considering and serving the needs of others, without thought of personal interest or return. And second, the contemplative life, which must not be construed as an escape. . . . It is in the desert of loneliness and emptiness that the fear of death and the need for self-affirmation are seen as illusory. When this is faced, then anguish is not necessarily overcome, but it can be accepted and understood. Thus, in the heart of anguish are found the gifts of peace and understanding: not simply in personal illumination and liberation, but by commitment and empathy, for the contemplative must assume the universal anguish and inescapable condition of mortal man. The solitary, far from enclosing himself in himself, becomes every man. He dwells in the solitude, the poverty, the indigence of every man.

"It is in this sense that the hermit, according to Philoxenos, imitates Christ. For in Christ, God takes to himself the solitude and dereliction of man: every man."

Although Merton is writing about the solitude

and freedom of the solitary monk, what he says applies also to monks who live in community. They have also left the world of collective illusion to find God in solitude, and although this solitude is not as intense and unmediated as the solitude of the hermit, it is a necessary part of monastic life. Without it, monasticism becomes a kind of club made up of orderly celibates and little more. But community presents a paradox. In writing of Philoxenos's thought, Merton explores his belief that for the monk there is no law. There is something basic here, something connected to the fact that monasticism began as a lay movement, and involved a radical break with collective thinking. Given this fact, isn't there something contradictory in the rule of Benedict? Benedict became a monk in wild country, and when he received the monastic habit it was not a robe but an animal skin. Given this emphasis on simplicity and "the freedom of the Sons of God" how can you explain Benedict's rule? Why would monks need a rule at all?

Without getting into too much detail, it can be said that without any rule at all monasticism would not have survived. Cassian was one monastic authority who felt the need to put down in writing advice for monks, and this advice comes across as extremely practical. Rules are not limitations so much as they are time-saving devices. Why—if authoritative advice can cut through errors you will otherwise find yourself making— should you waste your time stumbling into holes other people have learned how to avoid, through trial and error? Authority here is terribly important, and its importance is a function of the radicalism involved in the monastic choice. Cassian compares the soul to a feather which is inert so long as it is wet, but once it has been dried it can float with any breeze; the breath of the spirit can move the soul, he says, only insofar as it has managed to get rid of all moisture. This freedom of response is contradicted at every turn, by overanxiousness, by scruples, by the desire to manipulate everything and everyone (including God); the simplicity, silence, and obedience involved in monasticism are designed to cut through these obstacles.

Benedict drew heavily on Cassian's rule in writing his own. More than any other source he relied on a slightly earlier rule known as the rule of the Master; many of the detailed accounts of proper monastic behavior in Benedict's rule come from the Master-source. What Benedict did with the rule of the Master, according to R. W. Southern, reveals his own creativity, his humane contribution to the idea of monasticism: "The difference between the two documents is immense. The Rule of the Master is diffuse, individual, and indefinite in its liturgical detail, where Benedict's rule is concise, universal, and clear. In the Rule of the Master there is much that is too general to be useful in common practice. . . . There was even more that was too particular to be of significance. . . . Benedict omitted all this.

He kept to the middle way of practical usefull-
ness, making everything as short and clear as
possible. . . . He seems not to have had the
searching and imperious spirit of the Master. In
his extensive borrowings he exemplifies the
humility which he urged on his monks, and his
briefest additions display the humanity he desired in an abbot. While Benedict's abbot was
above all to look after the sick, the Master was
more intent on discovering malingerers. 'Never
despair of God' says the Master; 'never despair
of God's mercy,' says Benedict, making a slight
but significant change. The Master saw absolute
obedience as a virtue to be attained only by a few
perfect monks; Benedict thought it was easy for
anyone with a serious intention. A comparison of
the two documents leaves an unexpected impression on the reader's mind. Benedict, the most
influential guide to the spiritual life in western
history, appears as an uncomplicated and self-
effacing man who was content to take nearly all
his doctrine from the Rule of his predecessor. Yet
with a few changes, omissions, and additions he
changed the whole character of his source. He
added strength where it was weak, tenderness
where it was strong, and terseness and simplicity
where it was diffuse and confusing. In so doing,
he transformed an already remarkable document
into one of the central statements of Christian
living" (*Western Society and the Church in the
Middle Ages*, Penguin, 1970).

It is not that the Rule of Benedict goes down

easily at all times. It is hard to read, with a straight face, about the dangers of laughter (though it is refreshing to see that every commentator hastens to assure the reader that the only forbidden laughter is the *wrong* kind, the ribald and distracting sort—in other words, the sort of laughter few people find themselves guilty of). And although the advice about children in the monastery—which in itself gives a picture of the times—is occasionally mild, it is disconcerting to read that children should be whipped when they disobey the rule. (This is typical of the ancient notion which survived until rather recently that children are simply miniature, unformed adults.) Despite these things, what impresses the reader is that the rule is constantly seen as a means to an end, the end being the formation of men who have done their best to see that the obstacles between themselves and God are cleared away. However harsh some of the advice seems, the mildness of the rule is equally impressive. (At one point Benedict says with grudging tolerance that although wine is no drink for a monk, it is impossible to convince anyone of the fact and therefore wine will be allowed, in moderation.) The middle way is always chosen, as opposed to the extremes of libertarianism and severity. The abbot—upon whom the success of the monastery largely depends—must "make no distinction between persons in the monastery. One must not be loved more than another. . . . A person of noble birth must not be put above another, form-

erly a slave, unless there is some other good
reason for doing so. If it seems upon consideration that someone should be advanced, let the
Abbot advance him, whatever his rank. But
otherwise let them be where they are, since,
whether slave or free, we are all one in Christ. . . .
Let the Abbot show love equally to all, and let the
same discipline apply to all. . . ."

The rule is the best place to see him clearly,
although Gregory the Great gives us another view;
his account of Benedict's life is full of miracle
stories, which serve to show the love his followers
had for Benedict, and also serve to illustrate
aspects of his rule. When Placid, a child who had
been placed in Benedict's care, fell into a river
and was carried away, Benedict—though he was
shut up in his cell—knew what had happened and
sent Placid's brother Maurus to save the boy.
Maurus ran to Placid, pulled him to shore, and
realized that he had walked on water. Maurus
claimed that this was due to Benedict's power, but
Benedict insisted it was simply the result of
Maurus' obedience.

Another story speaks of a clumsy monk whose
ungainliness caused the head of his scythe to fly
off the handle and into a lake. Benedict took the
handle from him, touched it to the water, and the
scythe head returned from the depths and fastened
itself to the handle. Benedict handed the tool back
to the monk, who was deeply ashamed, and said,
"Take your tool. Work, and be comforted."

Work, and be comforted! prayer and work, in

which people can lose themselves, to find themselves—these are the foundations of Benedict's rule. Work of the most basic sort is made sacramental, a kind of cooperation with the divine. At one point in his rule Benedict says that the person in charge of kitchen implements, bowls and plates, should handle them as if they were vessels for use on the altar.

It is this desire for the perfection of every aspect of life, a perfection which is the result of work offered gratefully, that is Benedict's legacy; the manner in which it is offered in the Rule is more important than any of the stories about him, or any single historical fact. It is interesting though, that he began his life as a monk alone in the wilderness, as a solitary, but felt at some point that it was his duty to help others live the monastic life in community. Why—if his vocation was initially to be alone before God—did he come back to human company?

Maybe part of the answer can come from looking to a very different tradition. Buddhism contains the doctrine of the bodhisattva—the person who is capable of passing completely into the state of enlightenment, the bliss of nirvana, in which he will become a buddha, but who for the sake of others hesitates on this side of that state to help others attain it. One story tells of a company of buddhist monks who reached a high wall. The first climbed it to see inside its borders a garden of unearthly beauty, and joyfully he jumped from the wall into the garden. The second monk also made

the difficult climb, saw the garden, and without
turning around to his brothers he also jumped in.
But the third saw the garden, and turning around
saw the other monks struggling through the world,
working their way up the wall with difficulty. He
had compassion for them and instead of leaping
into the garden he turned back to help boost the
other monks over the wall. Buddhist literature is
full of stories of monks and nuns and kings who
renounced their own desire for total bliss and
enlightenment until all beings could also attain it,
and they dedicated themselves to helping in that
work.

At the end of his rule, Benedict asks that the
"beginners" who have undertaken the life of the
monk to fulfill it "with the aid of Christ," as a help
"on the way to your heavenly country." Benedict's
rule is an encouragement to the singlemindedness
demanded by the gospel. Compassion led him, as it
led the bodhisattvas, to his brothers, and in his
chapter on "good zeal" he describes the community he hoped for: "Just as there is an evil zeal,
a bitterness which divides from God and ends in
hell, so there is the good zeal which separates us
from vices and leads to God and to everlasting life.
Therefore, let the monks practice this zeal fervently, with love, helping one another in an
honorable way. Let them bear each other's weak-
nessess—whether they be bodily weaknesses or
defects of character—with great patience. Let
them obey one another. Let no one follow his own
good but rather the good of others. Let them have

the charity and love of brothers. Let them fear God and love their abbot honestly, with humble affection.

"Let them put nothing at all between themselves and Christ, and may he bring us all to eternal life. Amen."

Chapter Ten
Catherine Of Siena

Catherine of Siena was a woman of immense authority in an age dominated by men, a loyal Catholic who had no hesitation when it came to telling the Pope his moral obligations, an ascetic who was known as an excellent cook and hostess, a Doctor of the Church who did not know how to write. She frequently perplexed and frustrated her family, and her own confessor did not know what to make of her. Her self-denial was extreme (it may in fact have helped to bring on her early death) and yet there seems to have been nothing of the puritan about her. Like Francis of Assisi, Catherine had an immediate impact upon her age, and helped to refresh its Christian understanding. Unlike Francis, Catherine lived her life very much in the middle of the secular world, and her followers did not feel that it was necessary to leave their worldly occupations to join her.

Catherine Benincasa was the youngest of twenty-five children. Her father was a prosperous wool dyer. From an early age she was determined to dedicate herself to prayer; at about the age of twelve she announced firmly that she would never marry. When her parents continued their attempts to find a suitable match for Catherine, she cut off her hair to show them she meant business. For years Catherine's relationship with her parents was tense. It was a contest of wills: They

believed that they could win Catherine around to a
more reasonable view of things; she knew better,
and at last they allowed her to undertake the life
she felt called to. She spent almost all of her time
in solitude, praying and practicing the most extreme forms of self-punishment: She beat herself, slept on a board, wore a hair-shirt and later
replaced it with a belt lined with spikes. She
forced herself to go almost entirely without food or
sleep. She left home only to attend Mass. For three
years she spoke to no one but her confessor. At
about the age of twenty she became a Dominican
tertiary, which allowed her to wear the habit
while remaining at home. At the age of twenty-
one, on Shrove Tuesday, Catherine had a vision
which she described as her betrothal; it marked
the end of her years of solitude. She knew that she
had to go to others now.

She grew closer to her family. She began to
nurse the sick, frequently taking cases which
other people found too difficult. Her reputation
grew. A group of people gathered around her.
They were known as the *Caterinati* to neighbors
(who were scandalized that this woman, known as
a holy person, would have strange men coming to
see her at all hours), and they called themselves
her "family" or "bella brigata," her "fine bri-
gade." They included an old hermit, who said that
he liked being near Catherine because when he
was with her he had more peace of mind and made
more spiritual progress than he had ever found in
his cell. There were also a number of clergy and

laypeople, merchants, lawyers, artists, poets and housewives. Though they came to Catherine for spiritual direction, there was more to their community than that. They referred to Catherine as "mama," and their affection for one another was apparent. Catherine—though she fasted almost constantly—sometimes cooked for them.

Many people in Siena disapproved of Catherine and her group. She was considered a fraud, a hypocrite, a madwoman, and the freedom with which she and her friends assembled seemed unbecoming in a woman who was supposedly given over to God. At one point this sort of talk led the Dominican chapter in Florence to ask her for an explanation of her behavior. Whatever Catherine told them apparently satisfied them. Raymund of Capua, later Master General of the Dominicans and Catherine's biographer, became her confessor, and through him Catherine won the support of the Dominican Order.

During an outbreak of the plague she and her friends nursed the suffering (several of them caught it; they attributed their recovery to Catherine), and one priest who knew her from childhood wrote that her help and conversation caused many conversions during this time. Catherine's efficacy in causing conversions was in fact so great that at one time three Dominicans were especially appointed to hear the confessions of people whose lives had been changed by Catherine.

Her effect on the politics of her age was also

incredible. (It may not always have been to the good. She was, for example, an ardent supporter of Pope Gregory XI's attempt to start another crusade against the Moslem conquerors of the Holy Land.) She was asked by the Florentines to intervene with the Pope on their behalf, so she went to France where, although she failed to settle the dispute between the Pope and Florence, managed to persuade him to return to Rome from Avignon, where for seventy-four years the Popes had resided, dominated by almost entirely French curia. (It is interesting to see the way some old Catholic authors write with horror about this state of affairs, as if it were God's will that the church be run by Italians. The Pope's freedom as a temporal prince was curtailed in Avignon, of course. This did shift the contemporary balance of power, but it was more a political than a religious issue, though the line between Church and State was not very clear in Catherine's time.) Following Gregory's death, rival Popes were elected, one living at Avignon and the other, who was supported by Catherine, in Rome. He was Urban VI, and like Gregory he was the recipient of Catherine's nearly constant stream of advice. She was able to tell Gregory that he was falling down on the job; she told Urban not to behave so harshly to his subordinates. Both Popes revered her. Urban asked her to come to Rome as an advisor, and she agreed. She did not have long to live, however, and shortly after she took up residence in Rome she suffered a series of seizures and strokes which

killed her. Catherine was thirty-three years old at
the time of her death, which occurred in 1380.

She was, to say the least, impressive. It is easy
to admire much about her, but there are several
things about Catherine which give us pause. Her
asceticism would appear simply masochistic to
most of us, if it were not coupled with her immense
charity and the joy which impressed everyone who
knew her. Even taking those healthier elements of
her personality into consideration we are put off.
There is no doubt that her extreme fasts, her self-
torture, her refusal to allow herself any but the
briefest periods of sleep, all brought on her early
death. She ate at the most only a few spoonfuls of
food a day, and during the last period of her life
her biographer says that she lived on the communion wafer alone. The fact that all her life she
intended to live with this intense devotion could be
seen as a mark of fanaticism—is it healthy for a
child to decide on such a life? We feel more
comfortable with converted sinners than with
life-long saints.

As far as this life-long dedication is concerned,
all that can be said is that occasionally some
people are marked almost from birth to be saints.
In our age Simone Weil, who died, like Catherine,
partly as the result of self-imposed austerities,
was acutely conscious of her strange suffering
vocation from a very early age. When she was five
years old Weil heard that the children of poor
miners were forced to go without shoes, so she
refused to wear shoes herself. Weil has been

accused of masochism and self-hatred, but her
spiritual authority and her influence on our age
are undeniable.

Extreme asceticism is difficult to understand.
Although self-denial of some sort is present in the
life of every saint, extreme asceticism has been
discouraged by spiritual directors from St. Paul
onward. (Paul told Timothy to stop being a tee-
totaler and to take a little wine once in awhile.)
Some ascetics—like Henry Suso—began their
spiritual lives with extreme forms of self-torment
which they abandoned later in life, in some cases
because they no longer seemed spiritually necessary, in others because they were seen as unhealthy. Rather than defend the extreme asceticism of Catherine it might be good to point out that
in the first place such extreme asceticism was
admired by many of Catherine's contemporaries
as a sign of the believer's dedication, and Catherine was a product of her time and place. In the
second place, to read Catherine simply in the light
of Freud could be a mistake; it might be more
important to read Freud in the light of Catherine.
The fact is that, in every religious tradition,
asceticism and spiritual insight go together.
Among the ancient Hebrews, the Nazarite was a
man who took an oath to live an ascetic life for a
prescribed period of time. Fasting and self-denial
are frequently used as methods for enlightenment
in the Hindu tradition, and although asceticism (in
the form of self-torment) was something rejected
by Gautama Buddha, asceticism in the form of

radical simplicity with regard to dress, diet, and speech form essential parts of the rule under which Buddhist monks live. Among several American Indian tribes, fasting and sometimes self-torture have been used in the pursuit of religious awareness. In several shamanistic religions, the shaman, before beginning his active life as a religious technician of sorts, spends time in solitude and occasionally in self-inflicted physical suffering.

It is cultural arrogance to believe that we can judge this pattern, repeated as it is in a variety of cultures, and in every age, from a superior vantage point. It is not that our own culture—especially our knowledge of psychology—cannot make a contribution here. It can; and one of the things it could do is help to sort out (as the best spiritual directors always have) the true from the false, the genuine pursuit of truth and wisdom from obsession and neurotic self-loathing. But if we begin by considering self-fulfillment, construed in the narrowest terms, to be the sole important goal in life; if we believe that asceticism is by definition unhealthy; then we will not only fail to understand something which is of permanent human importance, but we will also keep future generations from this understanding.

Our tendency is to see Catherine's asceticism and her charity as two separate things, as if she was an admirable person who happened, unfortunately, to have a few strange and extremely unpleasant traits which we are willing to forgive

her because of her obvious goodness. But in fact
the period of prayer, asceticism, and solitude
which preceded her public life was necessary to
the things we admire. It formed the basis of what
followed, including the basis of the one most
attractive facet of her life: the community which
formed around her, the *bella brigata*.

Catherine was the center of this group, its
reason for existence. She directed the spiritual
lives of its members, and her insight was remarkable. She was said to have the power to know
what they were thinking before they told her, and
was aware of their temptations even when they
were absent. She was in touch with them constantly. Since she could not write, all of her works
were dictated, and her literary career began on
account of her direction of the community which
had formed around her; she wrote to them, giving
advice, consoling, reprimanding—whatever was
necessary.

Catherine's role here, along with the powers
which attended it, may be hard for us to accept.
Autonomy is considered a modern virtue, but here
were people who put their spiritual lives into the
hands of another person with no reservation; and
whenever we hear of someone who is able to read
the thoughts of another we are skeptical. However, Catherine was doing what spiritual directors
have been known to do from the first centuries of
Christianity onward. The role of the spiritual
father (given Catherine's life we may see the title
with a certain irony) has been an important one,

especially in Eastern Christianity. The *starets*, or spiritual father, is "essentially a charismatic and prophetic figure, accredited for his task by the direct action of the Holy Spirit. He is ordained, not by the hand of man, but by the hand of God. He is an expression of the Church as 'event' or 'happening', rather than of the Church as institution. . . . While the confessor must always be a priest, the starets may be a simple monk, not in holy orders, or a nun, a layman or laywoman. The ministry of the starets is deeper, because only a very few confessor priests would claim to speak with the former's insight and authority." This definition, offered by Kallistos Ware (in *The Spiritual Father in Orthodox Christianity*, in *Word out of Silence, Cross Currents*, Summer-Fall, 1974), certainly applies to Catherine. Her confessor wrote of his reluctance to advise her. He believed that she was at times under the direct inspiration of the Holy Spirit. The stories of her insight into the minds and consciences of her friends are not at all unique. Many of the *startsi* were credited with the same phenomenon. Read Dostoevski's *Brothers Karamazov* for a fictional portrayal of a starets, Father Zossima. It is based on reality. Saints Tikhon of Zadonsk and Seraphim of Sarov were credited with the kind of insight Catherine was said to have shown. It must be a fearful thing to encounter: There are cases in which a penitent would be told, before he had opened his mouth, exactly what his problem was and what he should do about it. Kallistos Ware tells of a contemporary Russian bishop who was spiritual father to a number of people. One night as one of his disciples stayed awake late at night, unable to sleep because of his worries, the bishop phoned him from hundreds of miles away to tell him to get some rest. Our temptation to dismiss this story and the thousands of stories like it has to be balanced by the fact that they are attested to from the time of the desert fathers to the present, and can be found among the Hasidim, and those Hindus who stress the importance of a close relationship to a guru.

The *starets* is not someone who chooses the role for himself. Usually he is led through a period of silence and solitude to seek God—not in order to be a *starets*, but because that is the human vocation. Seraphim of Sarov turned suddenly from the life of an ordinary monk to the life of a solitary ascetic, and his self-discipline rivals Catherine's. After years in solitude he threw open his cell to all comers, and like Catherine he was able to see into the depths of those who came to him. Ware points out that the *starets* is never so presumptuous as to put out a shingle. People are drawn to him, and at first his inclination is to send them to another advisor. After a period of time it may dawn upon him that this is his vocation. The people who need the *starets* reveal the *starets'* vocation.

That vocation is, in the end, one of love. The depth of that love is the result of the preparation which is the basis of every spiritual director's insight and service, the time of solitude, prayer, and self-denial which can be found at the be-

ginning of the public lives of many saints—as well
as the public lives of Buddha, and of Jesus. This
process of detachment from the world, and then of
return to the world, lies at the center of so many
lives that it could almost be said to be *the* basic
religious story. Leaving the world becomes necessary—it is understood to be a critical need, and in
the time of detachment and self denial wisdom
comes: The Buddha said that during his medita-
tion he saw the making and unmaking of worlds; in
one of her visions Julian of Norwich saw the whole
cosmos, infinitely rich and varied and deep,
compressed to the size of a walnut; during his time
in the desert, Satan offers Jesus power over the
whole world, and the power is declined. The
power accepted by the holy man or woman is finally the power of compassion rather than manipulation, and it is compassion which leads to the
return. After years the *starets* opens his cell;
Catherine realizes through prayer that she must
go into the world. The Buddha leaves his solitude,
and Jesus goes from the desert to the people who
wait for him. For the spiritual father—or mother,
as Catherine was called—the point is that enlightenment is not a personal thing, an isolated
revelation. It must extend itself to others. It was
said of one Egyptian monk, "he possessed love,
and many came to him." Ware also quotes, in the
essay mentioned above, two other *startsi*. Seraphim of Sarov advised his followers, "Acquire
inward peace, and a multitude around you will
find salvation." And the sixth-century elder Var-

sanuphius told his followers, "I care more for you
than you care for yourself."

From the time she left her solitude until her
death, Catherine's life reveals the truth of words
like these. If the ascetism which she believed to be
necessary for the focussing of that love appears
repellent to us, we should at least realize that to
some degree it is part of the background required
for the rare sort of life she was to lead in later
years. Her love for her friends, for the poor and
the sick, was so deep that it is frightening at times:
At one point, when her confessor reprimanded
her for weeping aloud during mass, she prayed
that he would understand that some movements of
the Holy Spirit could not be so easily restrained,
and he received such a powerful sense of that fact
that he was afraid to tell her anything afterwards.
Her affections, for her confessor and for several
other of her friends, were deep and unrestrained.
People spoke of the happiness which was apparent on her face, and even at her most formidable
she comes across as one of the most attractive
people in Christian history. What was said of the
Egyptian *starets* could apply easily to her: "She
possessed love, and many came to her."

Conclusion

The saints I have written about were chosen not only for what makes them similar—their holiness —but for their differences. Ignatius seems like a fanatic next to Justin; Francis of Assisi looks radical next to Thomas More, whose life was light-years away from the life of Germaine. But this is part of the point. Without the saints we would enclose our idea of Christianity; their lives invalidate any easy generalization about sanctity except this: All of them took the spirit of the gospel to heart. John's preaching, in preparing the way for Jesus' coming, was "Repent, be converted, turn around." In the past there was too much emphasis on faith as a kind of membership: If you were a Christian it was assumed that you had it. The need for conversion, for trying to take these words to heart—even if it meant, as the words of Jesus indicate it does, that something must die in the process for something else to be born—must be stressed more than it has been in the past. It is paradoxical that the Protestants who stressed conversion most were those who also rejected the cult of the saints, and yet in the lives of each saint there is the commitment which conversion means, the total focussing of a life, the wholeheartedness which Jesus asked.

Throughout the Old and New Testaments the message is that God expects something of us, and that this expectation is bound up in the love God has for us, the desire of God to share the divine life with us. Given the depth of that love (and the height and the breadth, which Paul celebrates so ecstatically) we respond in a faint-hearted way at best. The idea that we are baptized into the death and therefore into the resurrection of Jesus, the idea that the love represented by this death and the life manifested by this rising are the love and life of God—these remain for most of us only ideas, interesting things; at best they remind us of certain ethical or emotional obligations: We must try to behave with a least a little decency towards one another if these things are true, and we must try to see life compassionately.

This is good as far as it goes, but it is not our vocation. We are called to a wedding feast, and asked to make the celebration real. The saints responded to God's passion for humanity in a passionate way. Their commitment was more than the fulfillment of a contractual agreement—they responded as lover responds to lover. Finally this is what becoming a saint means: It is simple, but it takes a life to learn. We are asked to respond to the words of the gospel in the spirit in which they were delivered.

Finding that spirit and learning to respond to it involve an openness to its manifestations. We can do this only by looking at the Christian past—in other words, by looking at Christian tradition. In this connection, it is important to rescue tradition on the one hand from the people who call

themselves traditionalists while treating tradition
as if it were something dead, and not a living and
therefore flexible language; and on the other from
Christians who insist on interpreting Christianity
in the light of the latest news flash from the
zeitgeist. Progressives frequently regard tradition, now that it has come to a point where we can
be conscious of it (as we could not if it were the
invisible informing thing it is in completely traditional societies) as a thing separate from ourselves, which we may judge without being judged
by it. Traditionalists act as if the self-consciousness which is the mark of our age had not also
marked them, and defend tradition as one unanimous unvaried thing, ignoring the contradictions
this involves them in—only one of which is the fact
that Leonard Feeney was not too long ago ex-
communicated for teaching what the Council of
Florence had declared a matter of faith.

We are living during one of those rare historical
moments which apparently mark the end of one
culture and the birth of another. If this is not the
case it is at least a prevailing illusion, and if this
illusion has become so dominant we should at least
consider it. Certainly we are living through a time
of extreme self-consciousness about the past—
both our personal past and our past as a people.
The passion for self-definition, and the attempt to
understand the place of the past in determining
what we are now and what we will be, make a
consideration of tradition necessary. One of the
necessities is the abandonment of narrow, defen-

sive readings and a movement towards enjoyment
and appreciation. Such an appreciation will necessarily involve the saints.

Traditions rise around human beings rather
than structures. To discuss Ignatius' idea of the
episcopacy or of martyrdom without discussing
Ignatius is a little like discussing various Christian
interpretations of the eucharist without mention-
ing Jesus. Ignatius' concept of religious authority,
and of the death he must die, arose because of
something *he* lived through, and which he believed
all of us are called to live through. Ignatius'
approach to martyrdom is worlds apart from
Thomas More's. More believed that to choose
martyrdom rashly—a gesture which became fear-
fully easy for him during several interrogations—
would be sinfully proud. He believed that the
proper course was to avoid it as long as it was
honestly possible to do so, accepting it as God's
will only when it became inevitable. The point I am
trying to make is that Ignatius and Thomas More
disagree—if what you want to do is lift a theology
out of their lives, leaving their lives behind. If you
want to find a *law* about martyrdom in either
martyr you will wind up confused: The rules
aren't clear. Embrace martyrdom enthusiastically
and without reservation, as a proof of faith to be
manifested to a dying world, Ignatius says. Look
out for pride and ego, More says; trust the inevitable, and accept martyrdom only if nothing
better comes from the hand of God. Both were
right.

There is a contradiction here only if you try to move away from the flesh, to make a law engraved on stone from something which is meant to burn with the fire which Moses saw on Mount Horeb. "Whenever the interior flame is lacking, there have to be commandments written on tables of stone. . . . If today we abstain from killing, lying, stealing, committing adultery, it is no longer because these things have been the subject of prohibitions written on tables of stone, but because someone has lived in a certain way and has died in a certain way" (Lev Gillet, *The Burning Bush*, Templegate, 1976).

I believe that this is the point from which we must now begin to see tradition. Tradition has become problematic for Christians because the battles which once gave denominational traditions a certain false life are no long being fought. Catholics have seen that what was once considered a changeless thing, a fabric from which no strand could be pulled without the whole falling apart, was really nothing of the sort. Protestantism, which began as a revolt against inhibiting and decadent tradition and appealed to the ancient tradition for justification, settled fast into a swarm of quarreling orthodoxies. Each tradition retains impressive qualities—the sacramental ideal, the saints, a long continuous and instructive tradition in the case of Catholicism and Orthodoxy; a refusal to compromise the Christian message, a razor's edge either/or approach to the Word of God in the case of Protestantism—but

neither, as an institutional reality, speaks very
clearly today.

What *does* speak clearly is the example of the
holy human being, the one who exemplifies the
spirit of his or her belief. John XXIII is a good
example; so are Mother Teresa, Helder Camara,
Dorothy Day and others who have undertaken
lives which are wholehearted and undivided. This
has always been the case: Benedictine spirituality
or Franciscan poverty or Methodism or Quaker
spirituality begin not with rules and regulations,
but with Benedict and Francis and Wesley and
Fox, and the rules are at best means to an end.
The end is the confrontation which these people
were willing to accept. That confrontation is with
the living God we claim to believe in.

What it would mean to fall into the hands of the
living God, and not the God we have ideas about,
is something we can begin to learn by looking at
the lives of the saints. We might at least be
relieved of the illusion that our time is peculiarly
difficult for Christians. The assumption behind
this notion is that there were times which were
easy, and that once, being a Christian was simple:
Obey the rules and slide home. On the contrary, it
was always (like friendship, love, or anything we
really prize) a matter of self-surrender, dedication, graciousness, and learning how to receive as
well as learning how to give. Where it was real it
was always highly personal, like marriage. It has
never been easy or sure, and it is a terrible thing

to allow people to think that it was, or to let them
hope for salvation from a structure.

Even though tradition is not unanimous in the
sense traditionalists often suggest that it is, there
is a certain consensus about what Christians
should *not* do or try to be. For example, the weight
of tradition is in favor of a relatively ascetic life,
and against interpretations of life which make the
self a central consideration. The only self-concern
allowed is a paradoxical one. The self you are
allowed to keep is the one you find by losing your
life, or whatever it is you imagined to be your life.
However harmless and even logical self-fulfillment
may appear to be, the danger is that we will
accept the world's definition of what we are,
when our calling is to accept the name God has for
us, which only God knows—the name spoken of in
Revelations, where God gives to each of those
whom he has chosen a stone upon which is written
that person's true name. The lives of the saints
show us that there is no place we can rest easily,
including the unchallenging religiosity which is
self-indulgent consoling, full of bromides. Another
thing insisted on throughout Christian tradition is
compassion, especially compassion for the poor
and suffering. Even though it is true that Jesus
was not simply a social reformer, it is not true that
his message has no social implications. As traditional a Catholic as Frank Sheed has pointed out
that indifference to the needs of the poor could be
understood as "the answer to the question Jesus

was never asked: What must a man do to be
damned?" The single criterion for judgement
offered by Jesus in his account of the world's final
judgement is our behavior towards the poor, the
hungry, the imprisoned, the sick. Tradition emphasizes prayer, fasting, self-denial, compassion
—and rejoicing. What we are not allowed to do is
accept any divided allegiance—including an allegiance to one or another brand of Christianity.
The whole point is to try to hand ourselves over to
God, believing that the power to do this has been
given by Jesus, through the Holy Spirit.

When traditions crumble the thing which en-
dures is the life which traditions were meant to
exemplify. This, anyway, is what we believe if we
believe that God has the power to share that life
with us. The way that the saints responded to God
continues to instruct us. To say that saints do not
matter and that all we need is Jesus is to deny that
Jesus is the first-born of many brothers and sisters
—or it is to say that we, as we are, are all that this
exultant Christian affirmation comes down to.

The saints responded graciously to God's offer
of divine life. The only Christian past worth
keeping, as well as a clue to the Christian future,
is found in them.